Trapped Between Two Mountains

All rights reserved. No part or this book may be reproduced or transmitted in any form or by any means, electronic or mechanical, including photocopying, recoding or by any informational storage and retrieval system, without permission in writing from the publisher.

Published By:

M. PUBLICATIONS LLC

www.mpublications.com

Manufactured in the United States of America

ISBN: 978-1-945454-08-0

Edited by:

Andre Ricardo –
www.AndreRicardo.com

Copyright ©2018 Gwen Collins Womack

ACKNOWLEDGMENTS

My deepest gratitude to my sister Phyllis, who so willingly opened herself up to allow part of her story to be told. Her intimate recollections shed light situations I was not aware of in my absence from home. Thank you, Sis, I love you.

To my children, Pedra and Warren Collins, for loving me still.

Thanks to David Papillon for translating for me at the Florida Exhibitors Expolit 2016.

Very special thanks to Ms. Laura Harvey, lead reporter for the Madisonville Messenger. Thank you for keeping the story alive.

Special thanks to Andre and Juliette for believing in me. Couldn't have done it without you.

DEDICATION

I would like to dedicate this book to my brother, MICHAEL, for his unwavering commitment to help me. Whenever I needed him, he was there. I appreciate your wealth of knowledge and love you dearly.

***

I would like to dedicate this book to all of the readers of the first two books. Thank you for your support. To all the readers who can relate in one way or another; thank you for taking the time to read this book.

***

To my loving husband, WEST, thank you for loving me in spite of.

EDITOR'S NOTE

There were two things that struck me during this period of Gwen's life and it surrounds this idea of "Crossing Over." And, I don't mean walking before traffic or even a departure from this life. I'm speaking in terms of the moment you make a decision based on what is in your best interest. Some may also call this as *taking responsibilities for your actions*. This line is quite figuratively THE door to adulthood.

As you turn a couple of pages, you'll come across a saying that is quite well known in Spanish but not in English, but the idea bears mentioning. A co-worker of mine, Mrs. Dunia Rodriguez, told me the loose translation means, "You can drown in a cup of water." And, for a number of people we'll meet in this volume, knowing when and what to fight for can mean all the difference between safety and freedom or injury and incarceration.

Another idea that kept coming back to me had to do with this idea of opposition and its use in our lives.

Gwen has a few adversaries in this period in her life but none (in my opinion) that were pervasive and yet elusive to define as the one she had with Warden Velma Blankenship.

One time, as we were walking out of our American Lit class at Florida State, my professor, Ralph Berry was commenting on one of the characters in the book. He said to a classmate who was closer to the exit, "Aren't the villains the most interesting characters in any book?" And, before she could respond to his question, he laughed and said, "And, what does that say about our character?"

As I walked by them, I found myself sheepishly laughing at the irony because in fiction as well as real-life, we need adversarial moments to demonstrate what we know to be true.

Grab your popcorn and drinks because the exciting adventures of Gwen Womack continues.....

Trapped Between Two Mountains

A flashing red light came across the living room wall. The chatter from the women who sat on the couch came to a hush. Turning toward the broadest window, Gwen got up and spoke quietly, "Wait a minute, I'll be right back!"

Outside, two Pence officers walked out of the building to meet the three state troopers that pulled up.

"Oowww," She squealed to the women on the couch, "the police are here! Somebody's in trouble!" She walked around the wall until she got to the south door. She pressed her ear against the door, but could only hear the faint sound of police chatter and the sound of the P.A. coming from the officers' walkie-talkies. Gwen started to make her way back to the couch. "Oh, my god! Somebody's in trouble, I can't wait to see who it is!"

The door bust open. Standing in front of a crowd of blue uniforms was Pence's staff officer, Bowling. Bowling stood in front of maybe about seven armed troopers. Their belts were six inches wide with thick leather compartments all around. The left side held gray aluminum cans that had an aerosol cap on top. On the other side, behind the revolvers were billy-club sticks that swayed back and forth when they walked.

"THERE SHE IS RIGHT THERE!" Bowling shouted to the men in front while pointing at Gwen.
"She who!" Gwen said. "ME! What did I do?"
"YOU!" The policeman screamed at Gwen, "YOU, COME HERE! NOW!"

Gwen looked at these burly men, all approaching six feet tall and muscular frame. Gwen backed up. She backed up until she felt the wall and the fireplace behind her. As the policemen approached, she kept her eyes on them but felt around for something to hold on to. Her hand bumped the long, cast iron poker.

She picked it up.

Trapped Between Two Mountains

"What are you smiling about," Gwen asked Jink as he stared out the window.

They were in a car being driven by a white man whom they had just met in Cleveland just a few nights before. Jink's friend, Mittens and another woman Gwen hardly knew drove in his car ahead of them. The drive from Cleveland was uneventful. A far cry from the trip up north when Jink, Butchie and the women got high on the side of the highway.

"Are you alright," Gwen repeated.
"I'm fine," Jink said as he turned to Gwen. "You know, I'm missing my kids. I don't know why but I wanna see my kids tonight."

Trapped Between Two Mountains

"Jink, honey, I think that's great. But, Jink, we gotta talk about something. I didn't wanna bring this up in front of everybody but I don't have a place to stay. Remember, all this time I was at the treatment center then I left to see you and now we're back from Cleveland."

"Why didn't you say something earlier? I could'a got my people lookin' into it for you."

"Jink... I'm scared. I have no place to go and I know I lost all of my things."

"Gwen, I told you, I got you. Don't worry about it."

Both cars turned on to Summers Street and Butchie took the first of two parking spaces that just became available. When the car that carried Gwen and Jink slowly pulled into a space directly behind Butchie's car, Gwen tapped the driver on the shoulder,

"Slave, get out and open the door for Jink. He wants to get out."

"Yes, my master."

The driver got out and opened the door for Jink. Jink got out and began to straighten his clothes and pat down his hair. He glanced at his face in the outside rearview mirror when he felt Gwen brushing lint and crumbs off of his fur coat. Jink stood up and walked to Butchie who was now standing outside.

Gwen felt like walking over but she knew Jink's silence meant he needed his space. The men had a few words and from the look of their proximity to each other, Gwen knew whatever Jink had to say to Butchie, it was for him and him alone to know.

The men spoke very briefly, maybe two minutes, when Jink turned to the car, stooped and spoke to the women for a minute before walking back toward Gwen.

"Gwen, I gotta see my kids. Give me..." looking at his watch, *"give me about a half hour, not more than forty-five minutes and I'll meet you wherever you want for a drink or a bite to eat."*

"A half-hour! I have to wait that long?" Gwen said with a bit of desperation in her voice.
"I said a half-hour or maybe a few minutes more. I know what we gotta talk about, but ain't seen my kids in a good while. Look, let's meet at Candyman's and see where we go from there."

Jink shook his coat and started to walk briskly down the street. All kinds of thoughts started running in her head about a place to sleep, what was she going to eat, and where would she work. She just remembered that she didn't have a job to come back to. The thought of the crowd and noise and nosey people hearing her plight in Candyman's was too much for Gwen to deal with.

"Master, where are we going next," the white gentleman said.

Trapped Between Two Mountains

Gwen turned around, completely surprised that he was standing there hearing everything she had said to Jink. She also realized that he heard their intimate tone. Gwen now felt strangely uncomfortable in his presence.

"Jink! Wait!"

Gwen fixed her feet in her shoes and began to run after Jink.

"Master! Master!"

A voice behind Gwen called out. Gwen stopped and looked at the driver with an expression that conveyed she was being inconvenienced.

"Yes, what is it!"
"Master, what do you want me to do?"
"What do I want you to do? I... I... don't know. Wait, just a second." Gwen turned back to see Jink with a larger distance between them. "Jink! Jink, STOP!"

Jink stopped and turned around but only walking back a few steps.

"What do you want? Don't you see I got things to take care of?"
"Jink! Wait a minute... what about him? Can we meet at The Last Chance, instead?"
"If that's what you want. That's fine with me. I'll meet you there in a bit."

Trapped Between Two Mountains

With that, Jink turned around and continued to walk in the dark areas of the sidewalk.

"What are we gonna do about him?"
"I don't know. He ain't my concern. I'm lookin' after mine, you look after yours."

Gwen looked at Jink then turned around to see the man waiting patiently by the car. Behind her, she heard Jink say,

"Tell him to go home. I got work to do."

Gwen continued to look at the man, wondering what to do as she heard the sound of Jink's heels hit the pavement.

*** *** ***

It was only seventy-two hours before when Gwen walked with the two women into a gas station to buy something to drink and met this tall, somewhat stocky, mature white man.

He approached her in a respectful and genteel way, a manner that she noticed a lot of white male patrons had when they came by Miss D's place for a "date."

The issue of race was never a strenuous one for Gwen to deal with. She fondly remembered the crush she had on her friend's brother, the basketball player. But, there were others like the redneck hunter and his two sons who came out of the bushes and taunted her, Lila Mae and her friend. Lila Mae's words at the time, "Just don't say nothing!" resonated with her. When she asked her grandmother, Cecil, about how to react to whites, Cecil responded, *"When you feel the urge to smile, that's a good sign. When they smile back, that's confirmation."* For young people that might have been easy to do, but the people Gwen associated with a smile could get you into trouble and she found plenty of it in Charleston. But, this gentleman was different.

Gwen didn't want to be someone's master, just his friend. She saw something in his eyes when he propositioned her that she hadn't seen before: sorrow, and yet nobility all at the same time.

Nobility, not of the inherited kind but one forged through personal struggle. She didn't dare ask this man, who looked to be in his late 40's, what was his purpose in demeaning himself in front of Jink and the others, but she didn't have the space to ask him in private.

 As she walked back to the car where he stood with his hands to his side, she remembered Jink, Butchie and the two women laughing at him as he pushed ice cubes on the old, jagged and chipped hardwood floor with his nose. Or, the relentless names hurled at him from the people around the room. Somewhere down in her soul, Gwen knew it was just as wrong for them to assault this man for racial reasons as it was for that redneck family to verbally assault a single, black mother and two teenage girls for the same reason.

Trapped Between Two Mountains

*** *** ***

"Master, what would you like me to do now?

Gwen put her hand up, trying to gather herself,

"Sir, when they're not around, I want you to call me Gwen. That's my name, Gwen."
"But, Master-"

"No, that's an order. Can you stay right here? I'll be right back, I got to find Jink. Okay? Stay right here, I'll be right back."
"Yes, Master"

Gwen started to run down the street when she recognized what he said. She was about to turn around to correct him but she wanted to find Jink. Gwen ran up to every storefront and every restaurant, looking in the windows, but he was nowhere to be found, nor did anyone see him. Where could he have gone, she thought.

Gwen found herself in Frye's Alley and thought to herself, I'll have to talk to Jink in the morning. She had to secure a place to sleep. She saw her old apartment building but knew the landlord had disposed of her belongings.

As she walked between two parked cars, a mid-sized sedan, white with cerulean-blue colored doors. The vehicle stopped and a hand with a big, rubber cylinder was leaning out the window. A big, bright light shone in her direction.

"PLEASE STOP WHERE YOU ARE!"

Gwen covered her eyes to see who it might be only to discover it was the police. Without thinking about her condition, Gwen ran to the open field directly in front of her. Once again, she thought it felt like deja vu. This time she couldn't outrun the two guys chasing her and certainly not when she was expecting.

Gwen stopped running after about two hundred feet. She bent over and rested her palms on her knees and took several deep breaths.

"Why did you run when you heard us call you?" Officer Dallas Staples said.
 "I don't know," Gwen said panting heavily.
"All we want to know from you is where is Jink," Officer Harvey Bush said. *"We know you know where he is."*
"I don.... I don't" Gwen said between breaths. "I don't know where he is, I'm looking for him. I don't have a place to stay tonight."
 "Alright, come with us and we'll try to find you somewhere to sleep tonight until you can get on your feet," Staples said as he grabbed Gwen by the arm.

When they got to the police car, Staples opened the back door and helped Gwen get in.

Trapped Between Two Mountains

"I'm going to need your full name. We need this for procedural reasons."
"Gwen Collins. C-O-L-L-I-N-S."

"Okay, we'll be back with you in a few moments," Bush said as he closed the door.

Gwen sat in the back of the squad car. The hard vinyl seat was just as hard as the one that took her in for possession a few months earlier. It wasn't long before she also remembered the smell of a police car. It was all coming back to her now. Far from that new-car-smell, the backseat of a police car had an aroma all of its own. A hodge-podge of rancid odors that left a permanent thumb print of passengers before her. Their memories came drifting back like that of clothing that hadn't been washed in months. while. Just thinking about it made Gwen sick. She tried inhaling air from the front seat, but the ghost of prisoners past was pulling her back.

"Thank you, Jesus!" Gwen said as she saw Dallas Staples stooped down to look at her. "I thought I was gonna die in here. Can I get some water before we go?"
"I'm afraid Miss Collins, you may have to wait a little longer for your water."
"Why? It's hot and it's stink back here!" Gwen said as she inhaled the fresh night air that was now seeping into the car.
"Miss Collins, do you know anything about your time at the drug-treatment center?"

Gwen looked down at her feet,

"Yes."
"Did you complete your time at the facility?"
"No, but I can explain. You see, I knew that I wasn't getting the kind of help I needed and trying to find a treatment center that will actually help you maintain a clean lifestyle was my goal for leaving."
"We know why you left, Miss Collins and who you left with. The only question now is, will the judge give you another chance or will you spend more time in state prison."
"State prison. I ain't no criminal. I'm not. I'm just someone that needs help."
"Miss Collins, can you step out of the car for me," Bush said.
"But officer, I'm not a criminal. I just need help."
"Miss Collins, I'm not going to ask you again. Can you please step out of the car."

Gwen slowly crawled out of the car. Officer Staples took some handcuffs from his belt.

"Please turn around and put your hands behind your back. Gwen Collins, you're under arrest for violation of your probation."

Trapped Between Two Mountains

Gwen tried opening her eyes but the weight of her tired body felt like a heavy coat on her. She could feel her body but she couldn't move.

She heard noises, muffled noises around her but they were undecipherable. She also felt a throbbing pain in that area where her neck met her shoulders. She was familiar with this pain although she hadn't felt it since she was a kid. It was the pain of sleeping on a flat pillow.

The pain in her neck and the night's uncomfortable sleep forced her body to move on its own. She moved her hand underneath her head to fold the pillow in half. But, as in the days in Miss Cecil's house, nothing plus nothing leaves nothing and the agony of a restless night returned.

Why is my pillow so flat, Gwen thought. As she opened her eyes the cracks in the ceiling and the spec's of little bugs lying on the lightshade above her started to come into focus. She looked down and saw that she wasn't covered. Ahh, she thought to herself, that's why I felt so cold last night.

Gwen slowly sat up and saw several pairs of high heels on the floor near the chair that was by the window. Gwen thought that she must have been in a hurry and didn't know which pair that day was going to represent herself to the world with.

Before she could push herself off the bed to move her shoes, she reached behind her to rub the pain in her neck.
She recognized that she felt something stirring inside of her. It was an anxiousness that bothered her after she did something wrong or didn't do something urgent she was supposed to do but didn't and the consequences were about to visit her.

What's bothering me, Gwen thought as she tried to think what she was feeling, but her mind was blank. She stared down at her lap. She looked to the refrigerator. Did I forget to buy groceries? Did I pay the rent? Her mind was still blank, but her heart was racing.

The muffled noise that awoke her moments ago had returned but this time it was louder and more haunting. It was a sound in the hallway. A sound of heavy thumping on the stairs that led up to her floor. There was a rattling against the staircase railings and some shouting that came afterward. Whatever was happening, whoever they were, all of this commotion was coming closer to Gwen's door. Gwen hoped these people weren't coming for her.

Moments later... The noise stopped.

There was no noise in the hallway whatsoever. It was as if whatever was happening outside of her apartment just disappeared. So, Gwen decided to lay back down to try to get at least one hour of good sleep. She bunched her pillows underneath her head, pulled the cover over her and closed her eyes.

CLANG... CLANG... CLANK!

Gwen jumped up and saw a female police officer holding a baton and tapping it on the bars of her cell. Gwen sat on the bed looking around her dwelling, seeing herself in a small room. This was not the apartment she thought she was in a few seconds ago. Even the scent of the cell made Gwen think to herself, Oh, no! This is so gross. We need to get some kind of air freshener in here.

"Are you okay?" the officer asked.

"Yes," Gwen said softly.
"It's time to get up. Breakfast will be served in a half hour. Get yourself together because you have one phone call you can

make, so get your thoughts together."

The officer stepped back and began to walk away when she heard Gwen call her.

"Excuse me... excuse me, officer." Gwen stood up. "Do you know when I'll have my arraignment?"

The officer opened flipped over the metal cover of her notebook.

"What's your last name?"
"Collins. C-O-L-"
"I got it. Gwen Collins!"
"Yes, that's me."
"Okay. It says here that your arraignment is for 3 pm today. It would have been this morning but since you came in a few hours ago, they normally let you sleep and get yourself together before you see the judge."

Gwen said nothing as the police officer walked down the hallway raking her baton against the window bars of the cells down the corridor repeating the same message.

Gwen stood up and stretched. She still felt the pain in her neck though. She didn't remember coming into her cell. Nothing looked even vaguely familiar to her. She had only been there less than five hours. Gwen walked around her small cell looking at every inch of the few pieces of furniture the jail provided. This didn't remind her at all of her place on Court

Trapped Between Two Mountains

Street.

The mattress was barely an inch thick. It laid on a steel frame which was suspended to the wall by two metal anchors. Directly across from the bed was the commode, and in between the bed and the commode against the adjacent back wall was the steel sink. There were no windows and the wall was a gloomy charcoal gray, which perfectly matched the hard concrete floor. It was a long way from the Lang apartments. This was no dream for sure and her nightmare was just beginning.

   There was a dining room and large waiting area on the second floor that led to the women's holding cells. Gwen softly placed the food tray on the hard metal seat, the food looked just as threatening as the environment. She nibbled on a few small pieces of carrots before she got up and threw the tray of food out. She walked over to one of the guards and asked if she could-make her one phone call before her hearing.

The public phone was just a few feet away and next to the room where the female inmates were strip searched before being taken upstairs to their cells.

Gwen dropped a dime down the slot and waited for the dial-tone. She waited for just a second, pondering whether she should call her mother, Lila Mae or her father, Charles (or as his neighbors like to call him, "Chuck.")

Kanawha County Jail still had the older phones with the rotary dial and it seemed like an eternity for the last number to be registered, but the receiver on the other end immediately picked up.

"Hello," a heavy bass said.
"Hi daddy, it's me, Gwen"
"Gwen! My baby, how're you doing? How's my baby girl doing? They treating you alright at the center?"
"Uhmm... daddy, that's why I'm calling. I'm not at the drug treatment facility."
"You're not? You mean, they let out? Well, that's great news. You called to tell me you finished your time there. That's so won-"
"Daddy! Wait! I have something to tell you."
"Well, what is it, baby? Is everything all right? You need a place to stay?"
"Daddy, I got arrested. I'm here in a jail, here in Charleston."
"Jail! Well, what do you mean jail? How could you be in jail after having finished your time at the treatment center?"
"Daddy, I didn't exactly finish my time at the treatment center.... I left before time."
"You left before time? How... how could you leave before time? I don't quite understand."
"Daddy, I just left. I walked out last week and went back to the city."
"So, you're telling me that you became a fugitive."
"Something like that."
"How could you do that?"
"I felt like I was finished and didn't need any more help."
"So, you didn't finish your time and they went looking for you. How do you suppose I can help you?"

"I was hoping that you could help me get a lawyer. I don't have any money."

"I see. So, let me get this straight. You got yourself involved with drugs. The cops arrested you instead of sentencing you to jail, they gave you a break by giving you probation at a medical facility of some kind and now you tell me that you're grown enough to tell the police that you're done with your time?"

"Daddy, you're making it sound like... I'm a criminal...or some kind of fugitive from justice."

"That's what it sounds like you're telling me. You have a lot of nerve walking out of a place like that when they could have sent you directly to jail. What is the matter with you? Did you lose your mind or something? And, you think I can help you."

"Daddy, please help me. All I did was leave the treatment center. I didn't do anything wrong."

"You didn't do anything wrong. So, I suppose that walking out of a jail before you finished your sentence doesn't translate into breaking the law to you."

"Daddy, I'm not a criminal. I'm your daughter. Please, help me. I'm only asking for you to pay for a lawyer for me. I'll pay you back. I promise. I know I made a mistake but I won't do it again. Please, help me, Daddy, that'll be the last time I ask you for anything. Please, Daddy, help me!"

There was silence for a moment and Gwen knew that her phone call time was about to expire.

"Daddy... are you there?"

"Yes, I'm here."

"Are you going to help me or not?"
"I'm sorry, Gwen. You're my daughter and I love you. I don't have any money to pay for or loan to you for a lawyer at this time. My resources are tied up and it'll be some time before I see my way clear. I'm sorry honey I wish things were different. I wish you would have learned from the last time you had a run-in with the law but it seems like you haven't learned your lesson. Maybe this is the best thing for you. Maybe you'll finally learn that there are consequences to your actions."
"So, the answer is 'No,' I guess. Just like the last time."
"I'm sorry, Gwen. I think this is something that you got yourself into and I think you have to figure a way of getting yourself out. You're not a baby no more. You have to start acting like an adult. I'm sorry baby girl. I wish I could help you."
"Okay, thank you."

Gwen didn't wait for a response before she hung up the receiver.

She looked at the clock on the wall just above the phone. Her arraignment was in a few short hours. She looked at the phone dial and looked back at the second-hand rotating around the clock. She knew that time was working against her.

Gwen said nothing as the officer escorted her back to her cell. Tears slowly rolled down her cheeks. She wiped her eyes then laid on her bed. She brained searched for answers but none seems plausible. The weight of the matter made her feel drowsy.

Trapped Between Two Mountains

CLANK... CLANK. *"Collins! Collins! It's time to go."*

A female voice called to her. Gwen had been lying down on the bed with her hands clasped behind her head. Gwen got up slowly, slipping her feet in her blue and white tennis sneakers. She did her best to pat her hair down after she washed her face in the sink.

"You look just fine. Now, come on. I need to stop by the office and pick up the rest of your paperwork before you meet with the judge," the officer said.

After they went downstairs, Gwen sat in the waiting area just outside of the courtroom. She was told when she first entered the building that communications to other inmates outside of her cell's surroundings were not allowed. Gwen was reminded of this when she saw another inmate across from her. She desperately wanted to talk to her, and from the expression of the other inmate, the feeling was mutual.

Gwen's officer came back and told Gwen that they were going to wait inside. A few minutes later, another officer escorted the other inmate in and she sat a few feet away from Gwen. Gwen's officer gave some documents to the bailiff and went back to Gwen.

"Collins! We have a meeting in a few minutes and I need to leave to attend. I will be back in no more than 30 minutes. Your case shouldn't be called for at least an hour. I need you to be on your best behavior, especially if you want a lenient

sentence. Do you hear me?"
"Yes, ma'am."
"If you have any questions, wait until I get back."
"Okay."

Gwen watched as her escort walked out of the small courtroom while a guard stood near the door. The young woman whom Gwen noticed outside moved a few seats near Gwen.

"What you in here for?"
"Violating my probation. And, you?"
"They say prostitution but I was out for a walk minding my business."

The judge stood, brushed herself and walked out of the courtroom. The two women sat quietly as the bailiff put a stack of papers on the judge's desk.

A few moments went by when small talk between Gwen and the other inmate turned to despair when the sight of a new judge entered the room.

"Oh, my god!" The woman said as she covered her mouth.

Gwen was taken back by the look of her expression. Almost immediately a deafening silence fell over the room when inmates and supporters looked at the judge who fixed his glasses and sat down to a bundle of papers to his left. The mood in the room changed. Gwen turned to the woman who

Trapped Between Two Mountains

was now biting the skin on the side of her fingernails.

"Who is he? Is he someone famous?"
  "You don't know who that is?"

"No! Am I supposed to?"

Gwen looked up at the judge who had just tapped the bottom of a stack of papers to even them out in a pile.

"I don't remember his real name, but people in Charleston call him, 'The Hanging Judge!' "

Gwen looked at the judge then back to the woman.

"The Hanging Judge?"
  "You heard me, girl. They call him 'The Hanging Judge' cause he gives us more time in jail than he does the crackers."

The people in the seating area heard the judge say to the bailiff to bring the defendant for case # xxx up. The bailiff received the papers then walked to the center of the room:

"Case # xxx xxx xxx,
The State of West Virginia versus William "Boogie" Brown."

The inmate next to Gwen leaned over and whispered in Gwen's ear, "Now, some stuff is about to go down!"

The judge read the complaint in its entirety, occasionally glancing up to see Brown fidgeting, smiling at the people in the audience, making childish faces at the judge when he didn't think the judge would see him. When the judge finished, he tipped his glasses down his nose a bit and sat up straight.

"Is there anything you have to say about these charges, Mister Brown? By the way, why do they call you Boogie Brown? Is that supposed to be impressive to the ladies from your area?"
  "Your honor," Brown said smiling, *"they call me Boogie, cause I got all the right moves!"*
"Oh, really! Well, it seems to me," the judge said as he flipped through the stack, "that you've had quite a few moves that have gotten you locked up in the past. You have a prison record that dates back to when you were sixteen. This rap sheet is quite impressive... burglary... burglary... drug trafficking... burglary... statutory rape. I see that was overturned on a technicality... extortion and drug possession. For someone who has all the moves, you've seemed to be less successful in getting away with your crimes."
  "Your honor, I've gotten away with far more things than you know," Brown said as his court-appointed attorney nudged him to be quiet.

"Your honor, my name is attorney R. Jones and I'm representing the defendant. Mr. Brown forgot to take his medicine this morning before this hearing and he's a bit delusional."
"I see," the judge said. "I suppose you want me to believe that he's a choir boy in disguise as well. He committed all of these known crimes and, by his own, admission, far more

crimes than the court or police department are aware of."
"No, your honor. What I am saying is that Mister Brown misspoke."

"No, I didn't!" Brown blurted out as he thumped his chest. "I'm a man, I made a mistake and I'm here to pay my debt to society so I can get back to my life."

"I see...uhh Mister Brown. You think is just a walk in the park. That you can burglarize a home and threaten the home owner and I'll just go easy on you because of prison overcrowding, huh"

"Your honor-"

"I'm not finished, Mister Brown. I've had just enough of your childish demeanor, bombastic and petulance stance with this court. I've heard enough. It is the opinion of this court that a lengthy sentence is due in order for you to learn the meaning of repentance and contrition. You will not develop these traits on your own and I don't suspect you would find yourself in any self-regulating religious institution for spiritual guidance. So, I hereby sentence you to 10 years in the State penitentiary. And, I hope for your sake, Mister Boogie Brown, that you shed yourself of these limiting personality traits that have thus far been a detriment to your development. You may go now."

Just as the guard approached Brown to escort him from his attorney, Brown turned back to the judge who was now looking at the next lot of papers.

"Excuse me your honor, I want to thank you for believing that

ten years will bring about a change in my behavior, but I'll be out in no time. I can do ten years standing on my head!"

The judge, who was now sitting upright took off his glasses from his face and smiled at him.

"Oh, really? Well here's another ten years to help you stand upright again. Take this fool out of my court, right now!"

Gwen had her hand placed over her mouth almost the entire time the interaction went down. Before she could say anything to the woman beside her, she turned around and saw a young man next to her-extending his hand.

"Hi, Gwen Collins? You can call me, Ralph. I'm your court-appointed attorney. Just relax and leave everything up to me. I'm sorry I was late, my car broke down and it was difficult to get parking. Don't worry, I've had a chance to read up on your case and I'm going to appeal for leniency since there's really no defense for willfully breaking probation. Is that alright with you?"

Gwen thought about what had just been said and what seemed to be her lawyer saying, just give up.

"Is that the best you can do? I mean, I don't want to go to jail."
    "Miss Collins. You left... or you ran away from a simple drug-rehabilitation program. While everybody else was charge with a felony. Can I offer you a bit of advice to you?"

"Advice! Is that all you have is advice? What about strategy? What about a technicality? Why don't we try to get me off on a technicality?"

"Miss Collins. There's nothing extenuating about what you did. You violated your probation on your own accord. You admitted that you, on your own, left the facility at a time when you knew there were few guards present. The judge has this information. Let's play, 'The Honesty card' as a defense."

"Honesty?"

"Honesty! The judge is already upset and frustrated by the last guy who came through here. It's 4:15, and he's cranky. He's ready to go home, get some dinner, watch the game and put these cases behind him. Do you really want to play the wrong card with this judge?"

"No, I suppose not. But, there's no other choice for me?"

"This would be your first conviction. The judge tends to go lighter on first-timers to send a message and try to discourage past behaviors. They don't want to be shown up in their courtrooms by the likes of Boogie Browns. Let's go in humbly and explain what was going on at the time and appeal for leniency for a first timer and for youthful indiscretion. Are you with me on this?"

Gwen nodded and then turned as the bailiff was reading the court case number that Gwen knew was about to have her name attached to this recital. A few seconds later, the words, "The State of West Virginia Versus Gwen Collins," came out of the mouth of the bailiff. Gwen walked through the aisle with her lawyer and stood in front of the judge with her hands to the side. The judge, as before, read all of the charges then looked

Trapped Between Two Mountains

at Gwen.

"Miss Collins... I'm reading this complaint and looking at you but I can't reconcile these charges with the person standing right in front of me. You don't look like someone who would do these things. Am I missing something or are you standing in for someone else?"

"No, your honor. I am so sorry. I made a mistake. I shouldn't have left the treatment center. I thought I was ready. I thought I was making an intelligent decision by leaving early because I had gotten the treatment I needed."

"But, Miss Collins, it also states here that you were given fair warning not to go anywhere near this Jink. If this is the same Jink whose been in my court numerous times in the past, then I am confident that you have been doing more than just abusing narcotics. Have you been doing things with or for Jink that is unrelated to drug use and against the law, Miss Collins?"

"No, sir."

"Miss Collins. I see this all the time: a woman's in love. She'll do anything for her man and she'll be anything for her man. But, Miss Collins, this man is no good. It says here that you're from Kentucky and that you recently graduated from the Job Corps. Miss Collins, you have so much going for you. Why do you want to throw it all away for a man like this?"

"Your honor. I need help. Please don't send me to prison. I promise I won't go anywhere near him again. I promise. Please don't send me to jail. Send me back to the Treatment Center. I'll go. I'll go now. In fact, I'll walk back."

"Miss Collins, it says here that you promised the exact same thing at the probationary hearing a couple of months ago.

Trapped Between Two Mountains

What would make this any different?"
"Your honor, I'm a changed woman. Please give me a chance. Please!"

The judge stared at Gwen and looked at the tears flowing down her cheeks.

"Miss Collins, I'm afraid that if I send you back to the Treatment Center, you'll find a way to leave there and go dillydallying with Jink. I don't think that you've truly given him up in your heart. I've been meaning to ask you. Where were you all this time when you left the Treatment Center and when the police found you walking through Frye's Alley at 2 a.m. last night?"

Gwen stared at him and said nothing.

"Who were you with, Miss Collins?"

Gwen said nothing.

"Okay, Miss Collins, it's clear to me that you are unable to make a true commitment to change without it involving Jink. So, I'm going to sentence you to a place where I know you'll be instructed in the best possible way to learn independence and self-respect. Miss Collins, I'm sentencing you to a minimum of one year to a maximum of fifteen years in Pence State Prison. This is a minimum-security prison. Since you've accrued 327 days good time in jail and in the Guthrie Treatment Center...

with time served, you should be eligible for parole in a few months. That's if... if, you comply with the rules."

"But, your honor, I only left the Treatment Center. Why can't you send me back and give me more time."
"I wish I could Miss Collins. You look like a nice person who got involved with the wrong crowd. Hopefully, your time at this place will enable you to think clearly and plot out a new path from your life and one that doesn't involve drugs and alcohol. And... one that doesn't involve Jink."

Trapped Between Two Mountains

"Inmate Collins!"

Gwen sat on her bed with her eyes closed singing a Motown song when she heard her name called again.

"Inmate Collins, it's time to go!"

 The person behind those words was Officer O'Hara, a somber and slim, blond officer whose had very few words for Gwen since she came, and even less eye contact.

"Gather all of your belongings and place them in a pile right over here by this side of the cell. My partner will check for any kind any of contraband. This is routine. Inmate, I need you to *raise your hands to the ceiling and look forward. Try not to move. "*

As hard as it was for Gwen not to move as she was being patted down, she couldn't resist the urge to look over to the male officer who was meticulously going through the small bag of things she had. He was wearing a thin pair of surgical gloves and slowly examining every article very closely. From an angle, Gwen saw the badge of the male officer. Gwen waited a moment when O'Hara was looking away to turn her head in his direction. A glimpse of his shimmering badge revealed the name, Hernandez.

His coffee-colored complexion and his small rings of curly black hair had momentarily intrigued her. Was he Cuban? Was he Dominican? Was he Puerto Rican? This was the first time she had ever come into contact with a Latin man. She heard quite a few things about the romantic Latin male. She heard they were men of mystery, the tall-dark-and-handsome type.

He didn't say a word directly to Gwen but softly grumbled something into O'Hara's ear as he walked by and waited outside the cell. Gwen was still looking straight ahead although O'Hara allowed her to lower her hands. Looking forward didn't mean Gwen couldn't shift her eyes to the left.

"Inmate Collins!"

Gwen immediately turned to the opposite direction only to notice that O'Hara had caught her. O'Hara said nothing for a second then handed Gwen her bag of clothes.

"We have to stop by the office downstairs to sign a few papers and pick up your transfer papers."

"Inmate Collins before we leave the building," O'Hara uttered as she reached to the side of the wide leather belt, removing a pair of metal handcuffs from its leather holster. "I need to restrain you as a part of your sentencing. I see the look in your eyes but it is only a formality. I know that you wouldn't attempt to run away in the condition you're in but we still need to follow the rules. "

Officer Hernandez walked out first followed by Gwen and Officer O'Hara. Hernandez opened the backseat door for Gwen and only barely made eye contact with her when he closed the door. The police car drove out of Charleston to Summersville via Interstate 64.

This trip on I-64 was a lot different than the one she took just a couple of weeks before with Jink. The irony didn't escape her attention as she counted the mile markers and exit signs scattered along this long stretch of road. She stared at the patch of land that she, Jink, his ladies and Butchie stopped at to have a drug binge. Also, there was a row of Budweiser cans lined up against the yellow boundary line. Gwen remembered Jink's women guessing what message it was sending to the authorities about drinking and driving.

"Although, I haven't spoken much to you in the few days you were with us, Collins, I understand what you did and why you did it. I hope you'll learn from your mistake, Collins, because you are one of those inmates that don't belong in prison." O'Hara said after she turned her head to the backseat.

Gwen was surprised to hear that compliment, suspecting that O'Hara had nothing to say to her because of race. She saw O'Hara in a new light now.

"Thank you, Officer O'Hara. I really appreciate that."
"Our job is not easy and but most of us do it because we love our city and want to keep it safe for everyone. I hope you come back Collins and become an upstanding member of the community. That's all I'm going to say about that. Now, try to relax. We should be in Pence Springs in about three maybe three and a half hours. "

Gwen sat there for a moment until she couldn't resist asking the question that plagued for several days,

"Officer O'Hara, what's Pence Springs like?"

O'Hara took a deep breath through her nostrils and said,

"I'll tell you this. You're very lucky that you weren't in a different state. Where you're going is a very, very beautiful and quiet place. It really is like a country club... but it's still a prison.

"And, with good behavior, I think you could be out in about six months," turning to Gwen, "maybe even half of that. Who knows? But, it's up to you. My hope is that Pence is just what you need to get your life in order."

Immediately after saying those words, several garbled words came over their police radio and O'Hara and Hernandez listened intently. Gwen decided to let the conversation end there. It was the first bit of good news that she's had in a quite awhile. Somewhere in Gwen's soul, she knew what O'Hara was saying was true.

One hour passed and then another, but Gwen was unconscious of it as she slipped in and out of sleep. It wasn't that the backseat was comfortable or that the squad car was particularly quiet ,but it was O'Hara's words about Pence Springs being somewhat of a retreat that made Gwen feel at ease. And the peaceful sleep she lost finally returned.

As the police car slowed and made a sharp turn up this long, but quiet two-lane street. The path to Pence Springs turned to a small rural road. Columns of trees on either side of the street looked like cinnamon wafer cones and the mélange of green hued leaves looked like scoops of mint chocolate chip ice cream.

For the first time since her arrest, she began to think deeply about how her mother, Lila Mae would feel if she heard about her predicament. She worried that her mother would think she was a failure as a mom. And maybe it was a mistake to have allowed her to join the Job Corps and leave the safe confines of her home and predictable small town Madisonville living. Gwen was far less concerned with her father's opinion, especially after he told her that she made her bed hard and it was now time to lie in it.

The car drove about a mile more when Gwen noticed a big white house on the left. The house sat in a field with no other houses around it but a smaller house in the back of it. She looked at the porch and the rocking chair which was still in the warm summer air.

Just as Gwen was appreciating the beauty all around her, she felt bumps in by the tires running over something. A few more feet and more bumps, then they became more frequent. Gwen leaned up hoping to see what was causing the disturbance.

"Inmate Collins... don't worry. Just sit back and relax we'll be at Pence in about two minutes. These are just acorns; you'll see these so much you'll be sick of them in a little while."

The car pulled up to a gate on the right and an officer using a pulley opened the gate from inside. As the car turned in, Gwen noticed a double barbed wire that sat on top of the gate. The straight blades that were connected to the top bar looked to be a little bit smaller than the blades that stuck out from the looping metal band that was on top of it. Whoever thought of this, Gwen thought to herself, must not want anyone to get out. This place of refuge that the officer described earlier was looking more like a horror film.

The driveway lead up to a door circled around and led back out to the front. This was odd, Gwen thought, she had only seen driveways like this at hotels. The only thing missing was the baggage handlers. The car stopped and both officers departed from either side. Hernandez handed some papers to an officer who came out of the front door while O'Hara opened Gwen's door.

O'Hara put one hand on Gwen's shoulder and the other on top of the hood. *"Careful now. Lean back a little and swing your feet out, then push yourself forward before trying to come out."* Gwen did just as instructed and was standing before O'Hara.

Gwen looked up at the clear, blue sky. She turned around looking around at the environment. She saw discreet path that led to a hidden enclave of one of West Virginia's wealthiest communities. Their secrets were in eye-shot of Pence's windows.

"This don't look like no prison, Officer O'Hara. Does it to you?"

O'Hara looked around in wonder for a moment thinking about Gwen's question and realizing the irony of it all.

"No, it doesn't, Inmate Collins. No, it certainly doesn't."

Trapped Between Two Mountains

*** *** ***

The story of Pence Springs is an interesting one and in some cases, downright mysterious. Although Pence Springs is a euphemism for the West Virginia State Prison For Women, it had an innocent and idyllic beginning. The area was nestled between the Rocky Mountains in the mid-northeast area of Summers County.

Andrew Pence, a noted civc activist and businessman lived near Summers County in the mid-1850's. While visiting the area on business, Pence fell in love with the natural, fresh water springs and lush pastoral expanse, which was the pride of area's residents. Pence moved his family to this area around 1872 and made a deal to purchase the 30-acre property including the fresh water springs that crossed the property that owner, Jesse Beard, had in 1893. On that tract of land laid a farmhouse built just above and alongside the springs. It was here that Pence got the idea for a bottling company. Four years later, in 1879, he built a hotel on the grounds where the barn once laid.

Word quickly spread that this area, now known as, Pence Springs had a medicinal quality to it. No one knows exactly how the rumor got started, but it was said (and, largely believed) that bathing in the springs would cure cancer and almost every other physical abnormality. Wealthy vacationers flocked to Pence Springs for vacation in hopes of drinking just a single glass of water, which by this time had won a prestigious award at the 1904 World's Fair.

Trapped Between Two Mountains

In 1915, Pence died at the age of seventy-six. One year later the original hotel was completely destroyed by a fire. The newly redesigned and larger hotel commissioned by Pence's family was completed in 1918. This new structure, modeled after classical Roman architecture with wide, outdoor columns was the fashion of homeowners in the area. Pence Springs Hotel became the latest in that trend.

The hotel stayed profitable for the next several years until the stock market crash of 1929. A couple of coincidental events happened just a few years after. The Pence family considered several offers that were brought before them, including a pitch by Eleanor Roosevelt to turn the hotel into an educational institution for girls. Smaller, unreasonable offers, were dismissed for the 30- plus acre estate.

At the same time, the West Virginia State Legislature was mulling over the idea of having a separate prison facility for women that would have special rehabilitative and educational programs to help women reintegrate into society, with their families and in the workplace. The approved budget was $45,000. One agreement failed after another until Roosevelt's Finishing School For Girls, which had occupied the former Pence Hotel for a few short years dissolved. A legislator driving past the former hotel stopped in and the W. VA State Prison For Women found its new home.

One agreement failed after another until Roosevelt's Finishing School for girls, who had occupied the former Pence Hotel for

Trapped Between Two Mountains

a few short years dissolved. A legislator driving past the former hotel stopped in and the W. VA State Prison for Women found its new home.

*** *** ***

Trapped Between Two Mountains

"Okay! Miss Collins, please hold up the sign just below your chin and look straight ahead. Eyes forward please... thank you!"

Gwen's mind was blank as a bright burst of light temporarily froze her mind to any thoughts or reactions.

"Okay, can you turn to the side, your left side... chin up, you can rest your arms... take a deep breath... relax your shoulders and look at the red line on the wall... thank you. Okay, now let's get the other side."

Gwen stood still. It felt surreal. What did I do to deserve this? I only walked out of the treatment center. I didn't kill no one, she thought to herself. *"Alright, Miss Collins, please turn around and face the opposite wall. Again, take a deep breath... relax your shoulders. Tilt your head back just a bit... yes, right there. Okay, Miss Collins, we're done. Officer Smith will take you to your room."*

Gwen was escorted out of the room that looked and smelled like a high school locker room. The police officer didn't have a uniform on but was wearing a dress shirt and gabardines with a standard-issue police belt with multiple pockets and a badge-wallet clipped to the front. It struck Gwen strange, but oddly it made Gwen feel less threatening than even the county jail in Charleston.

The three women walked in a single file up the stairs to the second floor with Gwen in the middle. When they came to the top of the stairs, Gwen noticed a row of doors facing each other on the opposite side of the aisle. None of the doors had bars on them, only a lock underneath the handle. Officer Smith reached in her pocket and sorted through a cache of keys. After scrutinizing the inscription on one, she slid the key inside and opened the door.

Gwen walked into the doorway and saw the setting sun casting a path from the window to her bed. She looked around seeing the sink, a drawer and a toilet. For a space that looked like an empty bedroom, Gwen felt a feeling of relief that this was where she was going to spend her time. It felt something like her bedroom in her grandmother, Cecil's house in Madisonville.

Trapped Between Two Mountains

Looking at her watch, Officer Smith said,

"Dinner's usually at seven, so... you have about... an hour, hour and fifteen minutes to get yourself together. When you hear the call for dinner, come downstairs and wait by the dining room entrance. One of the guards will tell you where your seat is and explain the house-rules in detail. Then she'll most likely assign you a house chore."

Gwen lifted her head in surprise,

"A house chore!"
"Yes, a house chore. All of the inmates are assigned chores that they do during the day. That could be working in the kitchen, laundry detail or even working on the farm. It all depends on where they feel you'd do a good job. Now, don't get too excited, you only earn ten cents a day. It ain't much, but at least by the end of the month you'll have an extra source of commissary to spend."

Just as Smith was finishing her explanation, a tall, pretty blond walked by She turned in the direction of the officers to see who they were talking to. She smiled and did a quick wave on her way to her room a couple of doors down.

"Inmate Gaines!"

The young woman leaned out of her doorway looking at the officers.

"Yes, ma'am?"
"We don't like being interrupted by nosey inmates. Just remember, your stay here will be a lot longer than it needs to be if your manners are not in check. Do you understand me?"
"Yes."
"Yes, who?"
"Yes, Officer Brown."

Officer Brown! Gwen was wondering what her name was. At least now she had some power knowing the name of her captors.

"Do you have any other questions, Inmate Collins?"
"No, ma'am... I mean, no, Officer Brown. I just want to lay down cause I feel dizzy."
"Okay, but don't forget to come downstairs when they call. You don't want to go downstairs after dinner has been served. You'll have to wait until seven in the morning to eat."
"Okay, I promise, I'll get up."

"MEDICATION CALL! MEDICATION CALL!"

Gwen woke up abruptly. Her vision was blurry and she felt lightheaded when she sat up. She shook her head for a second and remembered the guard in the dining-room telling her that the medication call usually happens after the night shift leaves and the day shift begins.

Yesterday seemed like a blur to Gwen. She looked around the small but friendly room and remembered just twenty-four hours before, she sat in a cold, menacing cell with steel bars fencing her in. Gwen slipped her feet into her slippers and looked at the beautiful wooden floor, not the hard concrete that she awoke to for two weeks. This wasn't a bad situation Gwen thought to herself, no, it wasn't bad at all.

"LAST CALL FOR MEDICATION! LAST CALL FOR MEDICATION!"

Gwen quickly went to the sink and threw some water on her face. She scooped up two handfuls of water to gargle and she was about to spit it out when the face of the white girl who walked past her yesterday popped her head inside her door.

"Hi! You need to come cause they don't wait on anyone!"

Gwen grabbed a shirt from a pile near her bed, and wiped her mouth and sprinted out of the door. She followed the girl down the stairs and made the cue, which led to a small, older woman who was dispensing pills into a small white cup.

"Hi, we haven't met. My name is Donna. How are you?"

Gwen looked at her with a bit of shame.

"Oh! I'm sorry. My name is Gwen. I saw you wave to me last night when you were walking by."

"Hi, Gwen! It sure is nice to meet you. What're you in here for?"

"I don't know. They told me last night that they'd give me some medication that will relax me and—"

"No, no! I mean, what are you doing time for? Why did you leave the free world to come here?"

"Oh! Uhh... well, I don't really know why. I left the drug-treatment center against medical advice."

"So, you violated your probation?"

"I guess you could say that," Gwen said as she looked ahead of her to see how many people were still waiting for their medication.

"I don't think they'll say anything if we sit together at breakfast," Donna said before she popped the cup of pills and the cup of water in her mouth that the old woman handed to her.

As Gwen discovered the evening before, seats were assigned as Officer Brown explained, but as Donna walked by one of the guards and smiled; the guard pointed to a table by the window where she and Gwen could sit.

The dining area was lavish by any measurement of Gwen's experiences. The table near the window was perhaps the best place to sit if one wanted to eat and look out to the well-manicured field or to see birds fly around in groups, playing tag with each other.

"Don't be scared, Gwen," Donna said as she put a spoon full of mashed potatoes and gravy in her mouth. "You'll get used to this real soon."

Gwen didn't say anything, but drew lines in her mashed potatoes with her fork.

"*Do you know how to play cards?*" Donna said before she put another fork in her mouth.
"Do I know how to play cards? Not even Jink could beat me."
 "*Huh? Who's Jink?*"
"Oh! He's my boyfriend and the father of my baby!"
 "*Well, everyone around here plays cards and they play really, really well. So, you better be on your game if you want to play around here.*"

Gwen smiled excitedly,

"I'm a gangster when it comes to cards. My game is strong, I don't fool around."
 "*Okay,*" Donna said slyly, "*well, let me give you the rundown on who's who so you know how to deal with the right people.*"

 It took some time but over the course of several days, Donna was able to point out key people, cliques and people who had private connections.

"Currency," Donna explained, came in many forms. The key, she said, is to know was to know who did what and when, who had what and how much and who needed whom and where. Gwen told Donna that she was good at reading people and that she could, as the old people would say, "Throw a rock and hide your hand."

Trapped Between Two Mountains

By the end of the first full week, she had become acquainted with the mechanics of how Pence Springs operated. Her daily routine provided her with the opportunity to just look and listen. Some days, she would work in the field for a couple of hours; others days, she washes the lunchtime dishes. Everywhere she went, she learned Donna's bore truth.

Despite having the countryside at her feet and a converted hotel to roam as she pleased, not to mention three meals a day, Gwen found solace in her room and laying on her bed. She remembered herself as a young girl on her bed, looking up at the cracks in the ceiling singing Aretha's songs. But, there were times she was possessed with Gladys or Diana. She was a big Motown girl. Secretly, she believed she'd be the first female lead of the Isley Brothers. She clasped her hands behind her head and began singing Phoebe Snow' "Two Fisted Love" when a voice coming from her doorway interrupted her.

"Boy, you sure can sing. Where did you learn to sing like that?"

It was Donna peeking in from the doorway. Gwen covered her mouth.

"Was I singing that loud?"
"Girl, we all heard you down the hall. No one's complaining."
"I used to sing all the time. My grandma sang, my mother sang and I started singing in the church."
"What church in Charleston do you belong to?"

Trapped Between Two Mountains

"No," Gwen said, "Momma lives in Madisonville, Kentucky. That's where I'm from originally."

"I know you're different but I couldn't place where you were from." Donna came inside the room. "I've only been to Charleston twice in my life but I wasn't there long enough to meet anyone."

"There's nothing in Charleston. Where are you from?"

"I'm from Parkersburg. It's a real nice area. Family homes, manicured lawns and Sunday bells ringing in white chapels."

"Why are you here? I've never asked you."

"My mother wanted me to go to college. Daddy, too, but I had other plans. I'm here because mother wanted to teach me a lesson."

"Lesson?"

"Yeah, that's what she calls it. I'm here for only six months. I had to show her that I've learned my lesson and won't runaway with my boyfriend again." Donna sat on the edge of the bed. "Jimmy Don, my boyfriend, stole a car– he didn't tell me that he stole it– we had plans to go cross country and settle down some place like Los Angeles or maybe New York. But we ran out of money. We stopped to get gas and he told me that he was going to be right back and went to the clerk to get some cigarettes. The next thing I knew, he came running out back with a pocket full of money. We sped out of the station. The cops caught us two days later. When they decided not to press charges against me, my mother thought it would be good for me to see what prison life was like. So here I am being taught a lesson."

"Wow! I... I... don't know what to say."

"You didn't think that white people punish their kids, right?"

Gwen stared without being able to say a word.

"So, how long did they give you?"
"The judge gave me one to fifteen years but they gave me three hundred and twenty-seven days credit."

Donna giggled,

"And I thought I had it bad. Come, I wanna show you something."

Just as Gwen followed Donna out to the hallway, she noticed two inmates standing at the top of the stairs facing each other. Nothing seemed out of the ordinary as they approached them. Both of the women took a step back when another inmate came up the stairs. Like the doors on an elevator, both of the women took a step forward as if nothing happened.

The inmate who came upstairs stopped in front of a door and lightly tapped on the door in three different spots. The door opened slowly and the visitor pushed the door slowly. She turned and saw Donna and Gwen walking towards her. She stopped and stared at them.

Gwen and Donna slowly walked by the door and around the visitor. They saw the nude, intimate outline of the inmate concealed by the partially opened door. The visitor quickly walked in and closed the door firmly behind her.

Gwen stopped to take in what was happening when she felt a tug at her blouse.

"Gwen, come on. That's not for you to investigate."

Donna and Gwen made it to the bottom of the stairs, which was also the Main floor. Then, Donna walked towards a door down the hallway. Gwen glanced at the door but never really took notice of it.

Donna opened the door. With her free hand, waved for her to come. Gwen casually walked toward Donna fearful of seeing the officers working at their desks on both sides of the hallway.

"Before I show you what's in here, you need to know one thing... the key to surviving Pence is to keep what you know on the down low. Now, come on. I think you're going love what you see."

Trapped Between Two Mountains

The door opened slowly. What was beyond the pitch-black air, Gwen couldn't tell. She looked at Donna who had disappeared in the darkness in front of her.

"Come on!" Donna said.
"Come on, where?" Gwen said as she turned around to see if any of the officers or the warden was aware of their presence.
"Come on. Follow me! I have something to show you. Don't be a scaredy-cat."

With that, the sound of Donna's footsteps was heard walking away from her.

"Gwen! Let's go!" Donna shouted.
"Where are you?"
"Come here!"
"Are you sure?"
 "The lights are not working but the janitor knows that. I'm reaching for the light switch so I could show what's here."

Donna found the switch and a row of lights illuminated across the room. Gwen felt in that moment like she was standing behind the curtains of her high school auditorium and she was about to make her debut.

 "I come here just to get away. I figured since I'm leaving in a few days that you could come here if you want to get away from the crowd."
"Oh, wow!"

Gwen's eyes seemed to drink in every inch of the empty room. As she looked around, images of things started to appear in certain areas. She saw a piano, a radio, perhaps a place for seats in front of where she'd have her performances. This was a beautiful, blank canvas for Gwen. This room could be her stage and her toy chest.

"Does anyone know about this place?"
 "Sure, silly! But the guards let me come here to play the radio. Sometimes, I sneak food in here like Pringles or some Hershey's when I don't want anyone to see me with them."
"Oh, wow!"

Trapped Between Two Mountains

Gwen walked around the room, the echo of her words reverberated around the room.

"Oh, my gosh!"

"Hey, check out my radio, it also has a cassette player."

Gwen quickly turned around. Her eyes focused on the radio's cassette deck.

"Does it work?"

"Yeah. Sometimes, I bring my cassettes down with me. My dad bought me The Moody Blues, a John Coltrane and a Joni Mitchell. Did you hear her new song, 'Help Me! Oh, my gosh! I've been playing it over and over again."

"I think I heard it. Yes, I do know it! I heard it playing in a car that drove by. But, I didn't know what the lyrics were saying, all I remember is the acoustic guitar notes.

*** *** ***

"West, I was thinking about you all through English this morning. I didn't know if you were going to walk me to the bus stop or meet you at our secret place?"

"I didn't know if I'd see you either. How'd you get that note to me this morning."

"I told my friend to make sure you got my note. I did a favor for her and she did a favor for one of her other friends and so it went around until it got to that girl in your class."

"Yeah, I saw her looking at me when we got to homeroom," West said softly while stooping a little as to not let his head hit the back of the stairwell.

Sandy walked a little closer to West.

"I was standing by the bleachers watching you practice yesterday. You were really good."

"I was hoping you'd come by. I was looking around but I didn't see you. I was hoping that I'd see one your friends so they could tell me where you were."

"I came late because I had to get some notes from my pre-algebra class."

Sandy lifted up her knapsack and took out a small box and handed it to West. West strained to see the label on the box from in the darkness of the corner where he stood.

"What's this?"
"I saved up my allowance to get it for you."

West opened up the small box very carefully. When the lid sprung back, a sparkle of light glimmered from the side of a sterling silver ring. West lifted the ring from the box and saw the crest on top. Small diamonds surrounded the letter W. West slid the ring on his right hand ring finger. He stood there a moment and marveled how the dimly lit area behind the stairwell was just enough to reflect off of the small gems. He moved his hand from side to side and smiled as the light revealed the face of the setting of the stones.

"You didn't have to do that, Sandy. You know that I'm into you and I'm not thinking about any other girl."
"I want to be your girl, West. I want to call you my boyfriend."

West stared at her for a second.

"Why don't we meet after school where we always meet. I'll tell my friends that I've got to go to the store to pick up something for my Aunty."

Sandy leaned in and hugged West.

"I want to be your girlfriend. I don't like being just some girl you pass by in the hallway and wave to like those other girls."
"What choice do I have? I don't want no trouble."

West noticed that Sandy had her head turned away from him.

"I'll tell you what..."

West reached behind his neck and unlocked his chain. The fourteen-inch, gold-plated chain had a ring hanging from it. The chain sloped down West's black mock-neck sweater. He stepped behind her and draped it over her. He took his time, to secure the necklace. He felt her shiver a bit. He was just as worried as to what this would mean.

The recess bell sounded throughout the building.

"Come on, let's go. You wanna go first?"

Sandy looked at the chain that now hung from her neck.

"Why don't you go, I need a second to get myself together."

West kissed Sandy and picked up his knapsack but before he walked out from the backside of the stairwell, he stuck his neck out to see if anyone was around. He took three steps into the lighted area of the stairwell, as he proceeded to run up the steps he saw Misses McGillicutty, the vice principal standing just a few steps up.

"Excuse me! I thought I heard some voices down here. What are you doing behind there, Mister Womack?"
"Nothing, Miss M. Uhhh....I.. ahh. I got lost and I thought there was a doorway to my English class."

Misses M. had her arms crossed.

"So, you're down here for ten minutes talking to yourself and you don't realize that there's no door down here?"

Trapped Between Two Mountains

"No, ma'am."

"Who were you talking to?"

"No one, ma'am."

"So, if I walk over there, I won't find anyone around the corner."

West stood silent; beads of sweat started to appear around his temple. Misses M. lifted her head and looked in the direction of the hidden area.

"I'm going to count to three and whoever is back there had better come out or face three days of after-school detention."

There was no sound for a second.

"ONE.... TWO...."

Then the sound of steps was heard and Sandy appeared from out of the darkness.

"Sandy Bridgeforth. Well... well... well... What have we here? Now I see what's going on. Sandy Bridgeforth, I'm really surprised to find you here."

She turned around to look at West, then returned her glance to Sandy.

"Was West Womack doing anything to you that he shouldn't be?"

"No, ma'am."

"Are you sure? You don't have to be afraid."

"No, ma'am. We were just talking."

"You were just talking. Talking about what, may I ask?"

"Just talking. I... I... wanted to know if he had the same math book as me."

"So, you're down here on your lunch break in some dark staircase talking about math!"

"Yes, ma'am."

"Alright."

Misses M. looked intently at the chain and the dangling item on Sandy's shoulder.

"I notice you're wearing a very nice necklace. Can I see it for myself?"

"You want to see it?"

"Yes, I do. If you don't mind."

Sandy slowly took the necklace off and handed it to her.

"I see young people wearing them a certain way and I might be in the market for one for my husband."

Misses M. inspected it, every inch of it. Then she handed it back to Sandy, staring at her as the necklace left her hand.

"This looks like a ring on the chain. You're twelve and you're wearing an adult necklace?"
"I'm almost thirteen."
"Almost thirteen!"

Misses M. looked at Sandy then looked at West.

"Okay, I understand. I don't want to see either of you two down here again. This is no place for socializing."

As Sandy and West walked past her, he felt her cold stare following them up the stairs.

The vice principal's words stayed with West for the rest of the afternoon. "Was West Womack doing anything to you that he shouldn't be doing?" What did she mean by that? Why was she picking on us? We're not the only couple dating in school. I wonder if it's because we're interracial?
SZZZZZZZZZZ! The whistle blew. The coach let the whistle drop back to his chest.

"Okay, let's have two rows, left and right. When you receive the ball, you can make only five steps when you dribble before you make your jumpshot. The guy on the left-hand side gets the rebound and passes it the next guy on the right side and he goes to the back of the line. The guy who just made the shot now goes to the back of the line on the left. SZZZZZZZ! Let's go! We only have fifteen minutes left in practice tonight.

Trapped Between Two Mountains

Marzullo, pick up the pace, move your feet, son! You're not going to Sunday school!"

Near the end of the line on the right, West was third from the front and waiting for the ball to be thrown to him. He was the tallest and the only black student on the team.

"West, me and a few friends are going to head up to Court Street, thought you might wanna come?"

One of West's teammate said to him as he put his hand on West's shoulder.

"Greg, are you kiddin' me? My Aunty won't let me go out tonight. I gotta be in her house by eleven. Besides, I gotta find a ride home tonight. Coach said he couldn't drop me off near my house anymore. He said it was a favoritism thing!"
 "Come on, West. You always talk about your Aunty this and your aunty that. Be a man!"
"Be a man? We're only thirteen! Besides that, my Aunty don't play. If I don't wanna get my butt whooped, I'd better be in her house before she cuts off the lights. And, that's just being in the neighborhood."

A boy, several yards away tossed the ball to West. Because he was almost six feet, taking five regular steps got him considerably closer to the basket than his teammates. The coach was already sizing West up against the other schools in the division. It was in the Coach's mind, not a matter of the playoffs but what would be the school's ranking.

After West made the bank shot, he thought about what Greg had said and what he didn't say. He had heard about what goes on at Court Street. He would listen as some of his older cousins would talk the talk about the women they'd meet on Court Street and the inevitable aftermath.

West made it to the line on the left. He bent over, rested his hands on his knees and took a deep breath. He stood up and noticed the bleachers. Suddenly, he remembered the first time he saw Sandy standing there. Smiling and clapping every time he made a shot that went it. The bleachers were filled with his classmates but it was Sandy that stood out to him.
SZZZZZZZZ!

"Okay! Let's hit the showers. Don't forget to take all of your things. I'm not writing any notes to your teachers if you don't come to class with your homework done."

All of the players ran toward the locker room, West turned around and ran toward the coach who was walking toward his office.

"Coach...Coach...can I talk to you for a second?"

The coach turned around,

"Oh, West! Sure, sure thing. What's on your mind?"

"Coach.... uhmm, I've been thinking. I have to drop out of the team."

"You wanna quit! Why?"

"Coach, it's too far to walk home and... I'm scared about walking home at night and running into guys who pull up in a car and wanna start trouble."

"I see." The coach paused for a moment, looking down at his shoes. "I see. I wish there was something I could do but my hands are tied." He put both of his hands on West's shoulders. "Look, West, I'm gonna be straight with you. It doesn't help you to keep you in the dark. Look... the principal called me into his office and told me that it didn't look good that I'm giving a colored boy a ride home and no one else."

"I know, Coach. I'm not blaming you. I'm saying, maybe next year when I'm a full-fledged high school student. Maybe it'll be better."

"Well, what are you going to do for recreation?"

"I joined the Boy Scouts and I go to the meetings. We have a field trip tomorrow, but don't worry I'll try out for the team next year."

"You be careful now."

"Okay, Coach."

West took the long way home that night, constantly looking over his shoulders to make certain that he was aware of every car coming in either direction. He took the wooded areas and made his way to a fence that had a hole cut into to it by the train tracks.

As he walked through the hole, his knapsack got caught in one of the dangling wires. As he stopped to adjust his bag, he felt a sharp object bulging out of the side of the bag. He carefully unzipped his bag and reached in. He pulled up the box that contained the ring, holding it for a second wondering whether to make space in the bag to comfortably accommodate it or put it in his pocket.

He zipped up the bag and slid the box in his pocket. He carefully went through the gate. His watch read 10:30 pm. He looked at the street ahead of him. He knelt down and retightened his sneakers because his aunt's house was another thirty-minute stretch.

She tapped the point of the knife twice on the flat cast iron surface. The small block of butter slid onto the hot skillet and immediately the loud but familiar sound of it crackling and popping rushed throughout the house.

"Come on, now! Breakfast is almost ready. Y'all boys get up! Ain't nobody getting breakfast until you clean up that room and wash up!"

West's Aunt Minerva stood in the doorway of the kitchen looking down to her nephews' room. Then she wiped her hands on apron.

Trapped Between Two Mountains

West and his cousin Petey didn't need to hear her voice twice. The smell of frying pancake batter was enough motivation. Petey inhaled deeply detecting the faint aroma of sausage links right behind it. On days like this, West and Petey would jump out of their bunk bed and race to the bathroom. But, this day was different. West turned over and looked up to the ceiling.

"Come on, West, Aunt Nerva's calling us!"
"I'll be there in a minute," West said while turning to face the wall away from the door.

Moments before, West was in a deep sleep. A dream he had lived many, many times before. He saw himself standing in the principal's office. In front of him, a large desk with stacks of paper a foot and half high all around the edges of the desk. Legal forms scattered in the open spaces between. Behind the desk, a short, bespectacled, balding man in a white dress shirt, a black tie and a pocket protector with several pens sitting inside of it.

"West Womack, do you know why you're called to my office?"
"No, sir. I didn't do anything. I didn't bother nobody."
"No, son, it's not about you having any kind of conflict with any of your classmates." The principal leaned back in his chair and rocked a bit. He drew his hands together in front of him, clasping his fingers.
"West, I like you. The teachers have nothing but the best things to say about you. The coach likes you. Everyone likes you... and

that's a good thing. We don't like trouble and we certainly don't want to invite any kind of trouble around here. Do you understand what I mean by that?"

"Uhmmm, I think so, Principal Baker."

"West, what I'm trying to say is... I know that you have a friendship with one of your classmates. Ahhhh... let me see.... Oh, yes! Sandy! Is that right?"

Looking at Principal Baker a second before answering, West said,

"Yes, sir."

"West, I was young once too, you know. And, I had the biggest crush on this girl who sat to the right of me in my chemistry class. Boy, was she swell! Ahhh... nevermind that," Principal Baker said, then took a deep breath.

West looked down to his feet. He wanted to say something in his defense but couldn't find the right words. *What's the big deal about our relationship? I love her, she loves me. That's not anybody's business. Why are they picking on me?*

"West, as you probably realize by now, I was given a report by the vice principal and she tells me that she saw you and Sandy in some place where you don't belong. She also tells me that Sandy was wearing what looked to her to be a romantic gift. Am I making any sense to you, West?"

"Principal Baker-"

Trapped Between Two Mountains

"No, no, let me finish. West, you see we all have a role to play and my role is to make certain that my staff teach you a fair and balanced education. And, an education that will hopefully lead you to a profession that'll enable you to lead a morally and content life."

Principal Baker lifted up a few legal forms and placed a few into nice neat piles on top of a small stack of papers to his left.

"West, I have to be honest with you. I know that not everyone in every place abides by the laws of God, but we have to know that we don't accept race-mixing. Race-mixing leads to problems. We live good with colored folks around town, but it's my opinion that the races need time to get to know themselves better before they adapt to those kinds of changes. We think that people should stay in their places for the time being."

"But, Principal Baker, Sandy is my friend."

Principal Baker took another deep breath,

"West, you're at an age where you need to focus your attention on other things like your school work and on our school's basketball team. West... maybe after the season's over, perhaps when you're on summer vacation, maybe you can find a nice colored girl to have a friendship with. I'm sure there's a lot of nice colored girls in your neighborhood. Right?"

"Yes, sir, Principal Baker."

Trapped Between Two Mountains

Principal Baker looked at West for a few moments.

"West, I want to tell you something else." Principal Baker clasped his hands in front of him. "I had a meeting with Sandy and her parents in this very room late last week. They were quite upset with their daughter and with me for not protecting her. They decided to transfer Sandy to another school. What I need from you, West, is a promise. Promise me that you'll consider dating for another place and another time. Do I make myself clear?"

"Yes, sir."

"Alright, you can go back to your class now."

West got up from the chair very slowly and began to walk to the door.

"Oh, by the way, West... do you think you'll ever play basketball for our division?"

"Yes, sir... maybe next year."

West turned again to walk out the door when he heard his name called again.

"West! West! What's the matter with you? Didn't you hear me callin' you? Your breakfast is gettin' cold!"

Trapped Between Two Mountains

West opened his eyes and the blurry image of Aunt Nerva came into focus.

"West! West... are you feeling sick?"
"No, auntie, I'm just tired."

Aunt Minerva walked slowly to the bottom bunk and fixed the cover before she sat on the end of the bed. West sat up and held his head in his hands.

"What's wrong, West? You can tell me."

West rubbed his eyes and slowly pushed himself so that he was leaning against the wall.

"Does it have anything to do with you not playing basketball for the team?"

West looked at her for a second.

"Yes, ma'am."
"Well, are you just gonna sit there and not tell me?"
"Auntie, I don't think I'm ready to play with the bigger boys next year."

"Of course, you are. I've seen you play. You're really good, West. Can't nobody tell me different."

"I know, Auntie, but I ain't that good to play with the big boys."

"Sure, you can! What you need to do is to play with those down there by Washington Manor. If you really wanna be better, you gotta play with people who are better than you. That's how it is in life. You have to keep yourself in better company. If you wanna go to college, you gotta keep company with those smart kids. If you want to be a better basketball player, you have to go where there are better players and learn from them. You have to lose before you can win. That's just how it is in life. But, if you waste your time playing with those stupid boys around here and up the street, you ain't gonna accomplish nothin' but end up being a stupid adult. Stupid is as stupid does. You hear me, boy?"

"Yes, Auntie."

"If you play with them boys on Donnelly Street, you could be like that boy who grew up not too far from here..."

Aunt Minerva bent her head down and started tapping her lap.

"Lord, I can't remember that boy's name... Lord, what is his name... West, what's that boy's name? The white boy who just signed to play in the professional league.... I think his name is James, Johnny.... Jerry?"

"Oh! Auntie, are you talking about Jerry West?"

"That sounds like his name. Yes, yes, that's the boy I'm talking about. I heard my sister say something about knowing his family from some place up in town. Boy, he's a good player. That white boy can play some ball!"

"Yes, Auntie. I read about him in the paper. Sometimes, the coach would mention his name in practice."

"You got that other boy, he's real good too! Colored boy... he's real big. Big like your uncle, who lives down the street. They call him, 'Big Bo' or 'Big O'... I can't remember right now. But he's playing for the big team as-- Oscar! That's his name, Oscar Robertson. Lord, I don't know what's wrong with me. I'm having trouble remembering these names."

"But Auntie, you have a lot of good players out there. What if I make the team and we don't win any games. They'll say it's because the biggest kid on the team couldn't play."

"Boy, you can't play more than one position. You got to do what you came to do. You gotta have that self-confidence to show people what you can do. That's all you can do."

"Yes, Auntie."

"You feel well enough to eat right now?"

"Yes."

"Okay, now. Get yourself together. This afternoon, I'm going to go over there to the concession shop to see if they have some pants and shirts for you and Petey to wear to your Boy Scout meeting. I don't want them people thinkin' we don't belong. You, two, have just as much right to be in that club as much as anyone else. Okay, brush your teeth, wash your face and I'll have your breakfast covered up on the stove."

"Thank you, Auntie."

Trapped Between Two Mountains

Gwen was up early this morning. A sense of anxiety kept her awake most of the night. She knew when she awoke, it would be the last time she and Donna spoke, despite the fact that Donna promised to keep in contact with her after she left.

It was almost three months since she arrived at Pence Springs, but she felt extremely fortunate that Donna befriended her. Donna was only three years younger than her but she felt that Donna was like a big sister.

Gwen heard the thump of three knocks coming from the hallway or the other side of her door, but she knew it was the security personnel coming to escort Donna out of prison. A few moments later, Gwen heard the footsteps coming down the corridor from the right side of her room. As the footsteps were passing her door, she heard the voice of her friend on the other side: *"Goodbye, Gwen! It was nice meeting you. I'll talk to you soon."* Gwen heard another voice, a heavier one, but couldn't discern the words.

Gwen sat up and looked at the door, "Bye, Donna! I hope you get back together with your boyfriend!" Gwen walked to the door and carefully opened it up to see who was in the hallway, but she only caught a glimpse of the back of an officer. Gwen stuck her head outside a little bit more and at the same time in the space between the officer's limbs, she saw Donna's head. Donna turned around at that very second. They made eye contact. Gwen waved and Donna smiled. Gwen went back to her room and sat on her bed fighting back tears.

That long morning turned to evening. That quiet, lonely evening turned into a somber week. Before long, a month had passed since Donna left. Gwen figured if she hadn't heard anything from Donna within two weeks, she probably was not going to. And, she never did.

During that first month, Gwen started to take into account all of the advice that Donna had given to her. From the description of the warden to the personalities of the guards and the idiosyncrasies of the other inmates; it was all a part of the more the inner workings of Pence.

Trapped Between Two Mountains

The prompting by Donna to remember this, remember that and to keep notes, reminded Gwen of an old hobby she had when she was younger, but knew it would be useful keeping a diary now.

As Gwen started on her diary, she knew that it would be the one true friend that would never leave her. Gwen held up the diary one afternoon and flipped through all of the pages she had written in. She thought to herself that if she lived long enough, she would use all of her diaries to tell the world what she had been through. She'd press the diary to her chest just before going to sleep at night and would mentally say to herself, Someday, I'm gonna write a book about my life.

It took awhile but gradually Gwen felt comfortable walking around Pence. She engaged more with the other inmates and the guards offering small bits about herself after the obligatory salutations. Gwen noticed that the guards didn't mind the chitchat unlike most of the inmates who were slow to warm up, except for two guards: Officer Ward and Officer Crawford. Officer Ward a bit more than Crawford. Gwen noticed that Ward would offer little more than "Yes," "Okay," "Not right now" as her common responses; nevertheless Gwen noticed she was like that with everyone and she was always the first guard to leave when her shift was over. Still, when Gwen went to bed at night, she felt she was making some headway in Pence.

Trapped Between Two Mountains

As Gwen went about the routine of her days, she found herself smiling as she'd see certain people and would hear Donna's voice playback in her head. Gwen marveled at how perceptive Donna was and how accurately she was able to see people their peculiar habits play out. It was not unusual to see Gwen singing and making cassettes of her performances that she'd send to the Isley Brothers, Aretha Franklin or the Jacksons. It was that period where the guards would have their own spots where they'd relax or take refuge and it was always after Warden Blankenship had left for the day. The inmates themselves were also aware of this routine and made good on the time to get personal things done.

There was one time when Gwen and Donna were eating lunch and they noticed two women in line to get lunch. Donna nudged Gwen's arm:

"Shhhh! Quick! Look at the door but don't stare!"
"What am I looking at?"
"Don't stare! Look back at me. You see the woman with the auburn hair?"

Turning toward the door then casually turning back, Gwen said,

"Yes... and..."
"And you see the other lady there... she's the one... two... she's the fourth person behind her."

"Yeah. The one with the broad shoulders, side burn cut, salt and pepper hair?"

"Yes..." Donna leaned in, *"She's sleeping with the first woman and the first woman is married with kids!"*

"What!" Gwen quickly turned her head to see, when Donna pulled her arm.

"Gwen! Don't stare! You should hear them. They haven't been together in a few days so the tall one in the back will be expecting the housewife to show up tonight. She's due for some service."

"How do you know this?"

Donna sat back up.

"See, this is what I've been saying to you. See things, but don't see them. Use what you know to your advantage. You never know what keeping someone's secret will mean in a payoff."

"Wait. I don't understand. Why do I need to know this?"

"Gwen, Gwen, Gwen. You need things from outside, right? Like, commissary money or snacks or whatever. In here, it's one hand washes the other. If you can help somebody do their thing, they'll help you to get what you need. Got it?"

"Oh! I see."

"Look... over there. There, that black girl.. she's going to walk by the manly-looking one... wait... ahh...Gwen, don't stare! Look around like your not looking.... she's gonna hand her something. Most likely it's some pills that you take with coffee and it makes you feel like you're floating on a cloud."

"Oh!"

"Look...now.. see!"

"Now, what does she have to do for that?"

"I'll show you when we leave. Eat slowly so they have time to finish eating, then they'll all leave about the same time. The black girl is going to get something else from the other woman too. She's gonna share the pills with her girlfriend. Both of them are going to stand guard at the top of the steps. They'll just stand there talking about nothing.. but they'll keep an eye on what the guards are doing downstairs. If one of them comes up, one of the black girls will run down the hallway knock three times and come back like everything's okay. They'll try arguing with each other so that the guard has to separate them. That'll give the women enough time to separate."

"Ohhhh... now I see. I would see women standing at the top of the stairs and I didn't know why. I just figured they didn't want to be in their rooms."

"No. They're working. This is a business and all the women respect it as that. We have some women who need the time to make houch so they could sell cups to other inmates or make a few bottles to trade for something else. There was no need to sneak Bacardi into the building. Pence had its own brand. That's the way life is lived up the stairs."

*** *** ***

Trapped Between Two Mountains

Gwen discovered over and over again that the conversation she had with Donna that day was the way things really were.

Prescription drugs and a cigarette or two was routinely given without any discretion on the part of the night attendant in charge of disbursing pharmaceuticals. Inmates could request medication; and the attendant in turn would disburse a small amount, most likely two pills. The inmate would pretend to swallow after she received a small cup of water, but would actually just have repositioned the pills around the mouth. After walking away from the attendant she'd spit the pills out and dry it off before the casing disintegrated from the acid in the saliva. Eventually, the practice just lapsed into the inmate receiving the pills and promising to take them upstairs before she went to bed.

The pills represented one form of currency. The making of prison alcohol (houch or moonshine, as some would call it) was another form of currency. But, with the exception of a few inmates who were imprisoned for murder, the remainder of the women traded intimacy for companionship and commissary items. And with this arrangement, the inmates knew it began and ended within the walls of Pence.

★★★ ★★★ ★★★

Trapped Between Two Mountains

Donna and Gwen were the last to leave the dining room. Donna wanted to stay a bit longer because she didn't want Gwen to miss out on the entertainment, but they were rushed out by the annoying look of the guards.

They made their way out of the dining room. As they approached the stairs they looked up and saw two women standing at the top of the steps whispering. When they reached the top of the steps the two women took a step back to let them through, but the woman closest to Gwen took the added measure of staring Gwen down as she walked by.

Gwen and Donna walked down the hall and past the room that the tall, butch-looking woman stayed in. The door was closed but as they passed the door and heard the sounds. Both Gwen and Donna smiled, realizing that middle-aged housewives can moan loud, too.

Trapped Between Two Mountains

Gwen's first few months were rather mundane. Get up for breakfast call, obstetrics appointment on Fridays, working in the kitchen (as her house chores), mid-afternoon break, dinner time and then upstairs to play cards before the night call to go to sleep.

Sometimes, the warden would allow special events to take place; especially church services. None of the black inmates went to the church services because the preachers were from conservative, white fundamentalists denominations. But Gwen saw the opportunity to ignore the socio-political messages that often accompany the placid smiles and the weak handshakes in order to participate in the song service. Gwen liked the latter because she saw it as an opportunity to practice her singing in front of a different audience. Then, one day, an announcement came that none of the inmates had expected: the warden had approved of a dance class to help improve the morale of the residents.

Gwen heard initial gasps of excitement from the inmates, but a few minutes after the guards left, grumbling and skepticism set in. Some wondered what was really behind this gesture; others wondered if this dance class would replace something that the warden kept for herself and her guards. Still, a few others said something is better than nothing considering the warden always approved the gender-pandering, knitting class.

It took a few minutes for Gwen to size up the arguments (as if it really had any influence) and decided that a dance class could help build up her performance credentials. Since, some day she was going to perform with Gladys Knight and The Isley Brothers, of course, she could also showcase her dancing skills.

After her morning chore, Gwen walked into the dining room, she was a few minutes late and found herself in a line waiting to be served. She looked around for a different place to sit because her regular spot was taken. When she looked behind her, she saw the warden talking with Officer Bolling.

Gwen received her food, and as she walked toward a vacant seat, she couldn't help but to occasionally glance up at the sight of the warden and the guard talking. It was just as if

Donna was seated next to her. She heard Donna's voice telling her not to stare, and to be very careful how she presented herself in front of the staff. Then, reminding her: to watch out for the warden. Gwen remembered the whole conversation as if it just happened.

"Her name is Misses Blankenship and she sure does run a tight ship."

"What do you mean?"

"I mean that you better not cross her because she'll have you written up or have her guards write you up for the smallest of things to teach you a lesson."

"Why would she do that?"

"You like to ask a lot of questions. Just take my word for it. One of the guards told me that she's like that with them. If she gives them an order and they don't like it or they ask why, she'd tell them that she'll write them up for insubordination and it affects how much of a raise they'll get. There was one guard who didn't like Blankenship and Blankenship didn't like her and after about a month, Blankenship had her transferred to work at the insane asylum about an hour from here."

"Are you kidding me?"

"No, don't let her size fool you! Blankenship doesn't have any friends here. I was walking past her office and she was having a meeting with all of the officers and she told one of them that she's not there to make friends, she's there to make certain Pence is running smoothly. Then she told the officers if they didn't like her rules, they could get out."

Trapped Between Two Mountains

"Well, what happened?"

"Nothing. The officers kept their mouths shut and went back to work.

*** *** ***

Thelma Blankenship was, indeed, no joke. In fact, she never smiled and always had a blank expression on her face when she walked the grounds, talked with the guards and support staff and certainly not with the inmates except in those rare moments when an inmate was called directly to her office.

Mrs. Blankenship, was a woman pushing sixty, maybe early sixties at this time. But unlike Mrs. Smith, an elderly woman who was a part-time evening attendant who dispensed drugs for the inmates a couple of night during the week, Mrs. Blankenship was robust for her age. She was a short, rotund woman who was the polar opposite of the meek and frail, Smith. Blankenship was fit. Fit as a softball lodged inside of a small glove.

Blankenship always wore business suits, but something about the way she wore them gave the impression that she was wearing a military uniform. At about five foot five inches, Blankenship was one of the shortest women at Pence. She must have weighed between one hundred sixty to one hundred and seventy pounds, but even that looked like all muscle. She cut a striking presence anytime someone saw her, but, she did have a distinctly feminine quality about her. She'd like to go out around lunch-time in the middle of the week and have her hair washed and set in curls. Though she normally wore her hair with a coif in the front and the rest pulled to a bun in the back, whenever she would come back to the office with a slightly modified curl, she'd answer compliments to her hair with a silent nod.

*** *** ***

When Blankenship finished her conversation with Bolling, she left the dining room and walked in the direction of her office. Officer Bolling turning to the seated inmates and recognized Gwen; she gave a small wave. Gwen, in turn, put down her fork, smiled and quickly waved hello back.

*** *** ***

Virginia Bolling, by contrast, was by all accounts the most popular staff member at Pence. She worked the three p.m. to eleven p.m. shift. It was not uncommon as Donna once pointed out, to see inmates waiting in the main lobby at two p.m. for Mrs. Bolling to come so they could schedule a private talk time with her before other inmates flocked to her side. The first time Gwen recognized Mrs. Bolling, she was returning to the building after walking the grounds.

Mrs. Bolling looked to be between six foot to six foot, two inches tall. She looked to be in her late thirties. She had shoulder-length hair but she had that classic glamor of a Hollywood starlet from the fifties. She had that certain 'je ne sais quoi' about her that appealed to everyone who met her.

Trapped Between Two Mountains

She, most certainly had that Lauren Bacall-aura about her. She often wore formal blouses over an office-style dress pants and she always wore flats or a very small heeled shoe.

That day when they first crossed paths, Mrs. Bolling stopped and waited for her and Donna to reach the door before she extended her hand to them.

"You must be Gwen Collins. How do you do? My name is Virginia Bolling and I work from now until midnight."
"I'm fine! Thank you, ma'am, for asking." Gwen said as she received a firm handshake from Mrs. Bolling.
"Please, call me, Mrs. Bolling. I'm not crazy about being called Officer Bolling," she said as she opened the door for Donna and Gwen to walk in. *"Gwen, Donna knows this already but if you need anything or if you just need to talk, I'm here for you. We want you to feel comfortable but also to prepare you to re-enter society after you've served your time here."*
"Thank you so much, ma'am... I mean, I'm sorry officer... Mrs. Bolling."
"Mrs. Bolling! I'm fine with that. Please don't be nervous. We've all made mistakes. My job is to offer you a hand up."

Gwen nodded at the comment and continued to walk to the recreation room with Donna.

"See," Donna said with a smile. *"What did I tell you about Virginia!"*

Trapped Between Two Mountains

*** *** ***

Gwen stood up from the table with her tray when she heard a loud scream and rumbling outside the dining room door where Blankenship and Bolling just stood. The other guard who was also assigned to the dining room quickly turned and ran in the direction of the door. Gwen, seeing the commotion put her tray back down on the table and ran through the abandoned chairs that were by the other inmates.

There was a small crowd by the door looking out into the main lobby. Gwen stooped and leaned into a small angle between bigger bodies to see an inmate screaming and kicking while being held down to the ground by the security officers. She was apprehended by Officers Ward and Crawford while Officer Bolling knelt beside her trying to console her.

The inmate was screaming for several minutes in what sounded to Gwen like, "I see them... I see them... they were bleeding and running away... they were scared. God help them! God, please help them!"

Mrs. Bolling held her head up and poured a small amount of water into her mouth. The inmate took another sip and looked at Officer Bolling, "I saw a white man dressed very nicely in a white shirt, suspenders holding up his pants. He was smoking a pipe and he came out of that wall right in front of us. He was looking at me and he used his finger to call me over."

Trapped Between Two Mountains

The woman was hysterically crying and repeating a story about two young black men who came running through the wall and ran past her through the wall that led to the dining room.

Mrs. Bolling leaned over and hugged her as the woman's voice started to soften. One of the officers handed Mrs. Bolling a cup of pills and a glass of water. A few moments later, after the inmate was sufficiently calmer, the officers helped her up and walked her to her room.

*** *** ***

Long before Pence Springs became a minimum-security prison for women, the estate, like most of the estates in the South of this size were slave plantations. Within these territories lynching was well known, but what was not widely reported was the record of ghostly sightings decades and centuries after they happened. Pence Springs was notoriously famous for having residents, neighbors and tourists having similar descriptive sightings. The most common were the sightings of tortured slaves running through areas where walls stood and apparitions of former estate owners walking the grounds and or sitting on rocking chairs in front of the building that wasn't there.

Many of the inmates at Pence claimed to have had these experiences but when Blankenship received these reports, she took the files and locked them up in a file cabinet behind her desk. The inmates, via Blankenship's instructions, were given higher doses of medicine until the issue faded from the prison's conversations.

More often than not, it was the inmates who had field duty with Officer Ward that had experienced these phenomena. Blankenship always publicly chalked it up to heat exhaustion and nothing more. She always left explicit rules that these random occurrences were not to be put in their daily reports.

One of the guards confided in Donna that Blankenship didn't want any negative correspondence about Pence leaking out to the State officials. Everything was fine under Blankenship's watch. When Gwen was told this, she kept this as a watchword for Blankenship.

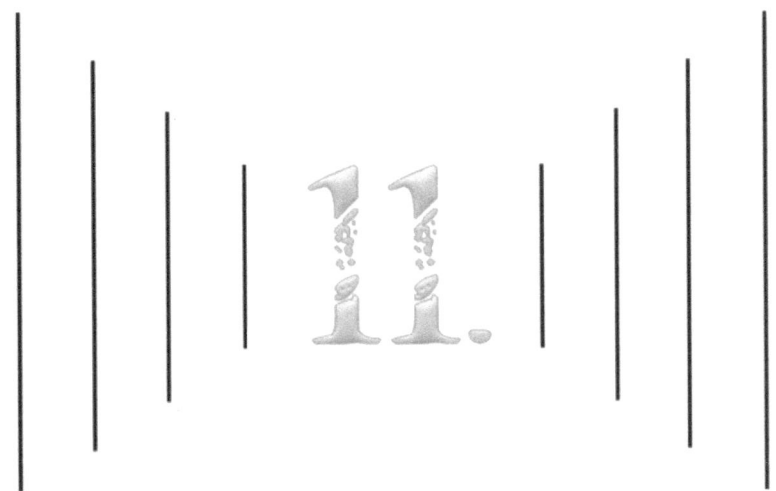

Gwen walked into the rec room still dazed from the incident that happened earlier in the day. From a distance, she saw a rerun of The Beverly Hillbillies airing on the television. Some women were watching, but others, particularly those from Charleston weren't.

There were a group of women in the front debating on where the location of Hooterville was. One of the older women, Ida, told her girlfriend, Jean, (also known on the floor as "Inch worm") that she remembered Hooterville being in Kentucky. Jean told her that she remembered two characters in Petticoat Junction talking about it being in Arkansas. But a woman sitting behind them told them they were both wrong. There was a character named Sam on Green Acres who said it was in West Virginia somewhere nearby in Pence Springs.

But, to some of Gwen's Charleston neighbors, the show's success represented the three W's: wealth, white and witty. Charlestonian life, the women felt, was world's away from the easy, carefree and uncomplicated life of southern or midwestern whites. The economies-of-scale would eventually shore up the fortunes of poor whites while neglecting the plight of Charleston's poor blacks.

These women, who sat in the back of the room, snickered at such a scenario.

Gwen, whom they looked at with suspicion and a tinge of scorn, represented a gullible version of themselves. Gwen, for her part, didn't need to ask why. She knew what not being from West Virginia meant: she would always be cast as an outsider, just one step away from being white. And, there were no keys offered.

Gwen didn't know where to sit. She wasn't particularly comfortable just anywhere, but she didn't want to sit by herself either. Then, she had an idea. She decided to casually ask everyone who was there something they wanted and she would try and get it. Gwen thought that things like snacks, leftovers or even magazines would be a good ice-breaker.

Trapped Between Two Mountains

"I don't even know!"

One woman said. She looked at the woman to the right, who then shrugged her shoulders. Gwen proceeded to walk to the back and saw the usual cast of characters.

 "Collins, what you want? Haven't you gotten yourself in enough trouble?" Terri said.
"I'm not here to cause problems, I just wanna be friends like we were in Charleston. Is that asking too much?"

Terri smiled and turned to the women beside her, whom themselves were snickering at Gwen's response. One woman spoke up,

 "You got any pills?"
"Me? No! I don't have any but I may be able to get some."

The woman looked back at Terri,

 "Yeah! That's how we can get some! Let's let Little Miss Sunshine get us some!" Terri looked at Gwen.
 "We wanna get high. You think you can get enough?"
"I think I can. I know they're gonna announce medicine-call any minute now. Let me see what I can do."

Terri looked at Gwen,

"*Make it happen, Collins! We'd be very appreciative of the effort.*"

"Okay....alright... I can do that. That works for me."

Gwen turned and slowly walked toward the door leading out of the rec room. It felt like a slow march to the firing line. What in the world made me do that? Gwen thought to herself, as she stood in the hallway just outside the door. How am I gonna get those pills? The questions flooded her mind, but the consequences also terrified her.

"MEDICINE CALL! MEDICINE CALL!"

Gwen looked down the stairs to see some other inmates lining up to the circular desk where Mrs. Smith was dispensing their medication. As she walked down the steps, Gwen realized that now would be as good as any time to get those pills. She knew where they were kept and it wouldn't be more than a minute to get them. The problem, she thought, was how to get Mrs. Smith out of the way long enough for her to do her thing.

Step by step Gwen anxiously breathed and exhaled through her nose. When she reached the bottom of the steps, she walked behind the last person in line. Gwen stared at the open door directly behind Mrs. Smith and each time she stepped in for something, she pictured herself walking in the room invisible to Mrs. Smith and walking out with the pills without any problems.

"Miss Collins.... Miss Collins? Hello, dear! Are you here for your medication?" Mrs. Smith asked.

Gwen didn't realize that she was next in line and the gaping space between herself and the counter.

"Oh! I'm sorry Mrs. Smith. Yes, I'm here for my medication."
 "Okay, dear. I'll be right back."

Mrs. Smith walked inside. Gwen's heart raced faster. She looked at the palm of her hands and felt the weight of the pills on them.

 "Okay, dear. Here you go... and here's a cup of water. How are you feeling today?"
"Fine, thank you. I had an issue with one of the other inmates this morning and I still have a little bit of a headache, but I'll be fine."
 "Oh, I'm so sorry to hear that. Well, just take two of these now and take one extra before you go to bed if you're going to be up late tonight. Will there be anything else?"
"No, Mrs. Smith, thank you very much."

Gwen held the paper cup with a couple of pills in it. She walked slowly up the hallway to the side and leaned against the wall away from Mrs. Smith's field-of-view. For a few moments, she considering the cost of her pledge and its worth at the possible expense of her freedom. Why would she do this and get a longer sentence maybe even a transfer to Alderson for who knows how long and for people she knew deep down inside would never like her much less be her friend. On the other hand, having some dialog could benefit her in some way, especially if she has to be there for a long stretch of time.

Gwen stuck her neck around the pillar only to see Mrs. Smith say something to an inmate and then turned around to walk back into the office. It was now or never, Gwen thought to herself. She folded the top of the paper cup then refolded the cup and stuck it in her pocket. She leaned against the pillar and moved her head just enough to see Mrs. Smith return. Gwen was surprised that Mrs. Smith was by herself this night, this was unheard of and Gwen took this as a sign from God.

She closed her eyes and listened intently to what she could hear from Mrs. Smith. It was a little difficult because there was a G.E.D class being held in the living room across from where they were. Gwen made out bits and piece of a conversation where an inmate was asking for medication for a certain kind of ailment and heard Mrs. Smith tell her that she has something just for it.

Mrs. Smith walked back into the office and came back out. She told the inmate how to take the medication while writing it down on a small slip of paper. Gwen quickly tippy-toed through the circular counter and into the office while Mrs. Smith's back was turned.

Once inside, Gwen walked to the right where a small closet was with the cabinet door open. There, on the middle shelf was the big, black, plastic bottle of pills the women asked for. While Gwen's heart rate would have broken the speed limit, she found it hard to breathe thinking about not having a second to waste. She picked up the bottle with one hand and with her free hand she unscrewed the top while still listening out for to listen for Mrs. Smith.

She poured a palm full of pills in her hand and quickly tightened the cap back on. She walked around the doorway and slid out through the outer edge of the door. She saw that Mrs. Smith was still distracted with the conversation. When she turned to the opening in the counter, Gwen stooped to crawl away from the desk.

"EXCUSE ME! EXCUSE ME! IS THAT YOU, MISS COLLINS? COLLINS! WHAT ARE YOU DOING?" Mrs. Smith had turned to find Gwen now standing up. "COLLINS, COME HERE RIGHT NOW!"
"I CAN'T...I HAVE TO GO TO THE BATHROOM!"

Gwen turned and ran for the stairs. She heard Mrs. Smith calling for her again.

"I CAN'T, I HAVE TO PEE!"

Gwen ran up the stairs, ignoring the voice screaming behind her and the voices of the women in front of her. As she reached the top of the steps, she extended her hands to the women whom asked for them. The women backed away and put their hands behind them. Noticing their refusal, Gwen pushed some of the women out of her path and made a beeline for her room.

She made it to her door and ran to the toilet. She threw the pills in and pulled the chain. The water rushed from the inseam, she smiled as the strong current created a whirlpool in the bowl. She was grinning from ear to ear except when the water finally settled, there was one pill left in the bowl. One pill. One pill that was glued to the center of the porcelain bowl. Gwen reached up to pull the chain again when a hand pushed her aside and reached into the commode and pulled the lone pill out.

"Miss Collins..." Mrs. Smith said panting, *"I'm afraid that you're going to be written up and almost certainly Warden Blankenship will place you into solitary for at six months for this little stunt of yours!"*

"Mrs. Smith-"

"Don't Mrs. Smith, me. You have a lot of nerve doing what you just did. You didn't think you'd get caught; and for what? Now you face extra charges and possibly more time here at Pence. I'd be surprised if they didn't send you to Beckley!"

"IS EVERYTHING ALRIGHT?" Officer Crawford said as she stood in Gwen's doorway.

"Yes, this inmate had the audacity to steal from the infirmary. We need to write her up. Should we take her to solitary now?"

Crawford looked at Gwen and was about to say something when she saw Gwen's stomach.

"I think we should let the warden decide when. We can't take that responsibility on our own. Let's just lock her in this room and wait for word from Blankenship."

Mrs. Smith stood up and looked at Gwen.

"You really disappointed me. I really liked you, Collins. You were different from the others. I see that I was wrong."

Mrs. Smith took out a piece of tissue and wrapped the pill in it and put it in her pocket. She stepped outside while Officer Crawford retrieved the key for Gwen's room. In a brief moment, Gwen watched the door slam in front of her and heard the sound of two pieces of metal rubbing together in the lock. The quiet was disturbed by the sound of receding steps of them walking away.

"Oh, I'm in trouble now. One month in solitary... three months in solitary... six months... a year! I can't do that, Gwen thought to herself. Oh, my god, what did I get myself into? How am I gonna get out of this? I can't do solitary! I can't!" Gwen began to cry.

KNOCK...KNOCK! Gwen held back her tears to listen to where it was coming from.

Trapped Between Two Mountains

KNOCK...KNOCK.... "COLLINS! COLLINS, ARE YOU ALRIGHT IN THERE?"

Gwen looked at the door, her voice cracked when she answered, "Yes!"

"Collins, what did you do?" The voice asked.

"I don't know. I did something stupid. Now I'm going to solitary when Blankenship hears about it."

"Well, what you gonna do?"

Gwen got up from the floor and walked over to the door.

"Who is this?"

"Perdue!"

"Oh, my gosh... Perdue. Thank you for coming to see me."

"Don't thank me. I just came cause I wanted to find out what you did. But since I'm here, what do you need me to do?"

"I can't stay here! Perdue, do you hear me? I just can't! I can't do time in solitary!"

"Okay...well... if we break you out, you'll leave?"

"Break me out?"

"Yeah. I said, if we break you out, can you get as far away from here as you can?"

Gwen thought about it for a moment.

"Yeah. YEAH! If y'all get me outta this room, I'll get as far away from Pence as I can."

"Okay. I'll be right back!"

Gwen heard some footsteps walk away from her door. She pressed her ears against the door and vaguely heard Perdue bang on doors and saying something that sounded like "Turn up your record players!" Gwen walked back to her bed. Her head was dizzy and she was now feeling nauseous. She softly drifted asleep.

BANG! BANG! BANG! BANG!

Gwen jumped up. The noise was unrelenting. She looked to her door and saw with each bang the wood frame trembling and the hinges budging from side to side.

BANG! BANG! BANG! BANG!

Gwen ran to the door. She wanted to tell them, whoever they were to stop she, was only kidding. But in between the banging of the door and her last reason to object, she thought about being in solitary. She thought about her physical well-being. Gwen took a few steps back from the door, hoping it would fall.

"STAND BACK, GWEN. IT'S COMING LOOSE!" Perdue screamed.

Gwen heard Perdue talking to someone else out there but knew it wouldn't be her girlfriend, Vivette. Vivette was too small and Perdue would never allow her "Mrs. Cleaver" type to do a man's job, as Perdue considered herself to be.

Gwen also heard loud random music being played out of the room. Gwen knew this was no small feat and one she'd have to fulfill especially with all of the effort being put into breaking her out.

BANGGGGGGGGGGGG!

The sound of the last hit came and the door knob and lock fell to the floor and rolled in front of Gwen's feet. Gwen was frozen for a second, barely cognizant of the music blasting from the other rooms down the hallway.

In a moment, the chatter of the other inmates screaming and the blaring boom-boxes suddenly ceased. It was as quiet as an old, empty country church before a Sunday morning service.

Gwen grabbed her shoes with one hand and threw the lock and pieces back on the floor. She looked out to thank Perdue but she was nowhere to be found. In fact, Gwen was astonished to find no one in the hallway; even the hallway in the opposite direction was free of inmates.

Gwen walked along the side of the wall, fearing the sound of steps would bring attention to her whereabouts. She reached the border of the stairway and looked over. She was about to walk downstairs but then wondered about an escape route through the rec area.

She walked inside. There was no one there. She was astonished that no one wanted to be seen outside their room when the officers came looking for her. Gwen shook her head debating whether her fellow inmates were cowardly or smart. The jury was still out on that. She made it to some double doors that were chained locked, but if the doors were pulled a certain way, it provided access to outside.

These doors led to a veranda that overlooked the side of the estate. There was a huge, old tree directly facing this side of the building. Several of the tree's limbs ran almost ninety degrees to the building. The limbs had grown to such an extent that it was easy to mistake the limbs for a bridge to the tree. The limbs this night looked like an invitation to Gwen.

Gwen looked at the path that the tree limbs were pointing to. She saw the possibility to straddle the limbs until she had cleared the barbed-wire fence that housed Pence Springs from their neighbors. So, she crawled on top of the limb from the veranda and as she thought about the direction, she looked down and wondered how far was the drop. Was it high enough to guarantee a broken leg or arm? Was it high enough to terrify her movement? Was it high enough that the fall would cause a miscarriage? Sure, it was a way out, Gwen resolved, but the consequence of a fall was too much risk for someone who wanted a lot out of life so Gwen crawled back onto the veranda.

Gwen walked out of the rec room knowing her only option was to leave from the main floor. How could she go back to her room? She'd never be able to explain how her door was broken down from the outside in.

As she made her way down the landing, she saw the janitor mopping the main foyer. He looked at her for a moment, then turned his attention to the space of floor in front of the living room where the G.E.D class was still going on.

Gwen didn't know whether to go in fear of the custodian reporting her. A few seconds passed when she noticed he continued to mop and pay her no attention. She knew she was free until the next roadblock. She looked around, and seeing no other officers in view, she walked out of the front door.

Gwen hadn't looked at the clock but guessed that it had to be between 8:30 pm and 9 as she passed the living room outside. The G.E.D class was still underway and the interactions inside shielded her as she made her way to the back of Pence's building. She looked up and saw the barbed wire wrapped around the top of the fence. It looked just as lethal standing under it looking up as it did when she was straddling the tree limb and looking down at it. There was no confusion as to what would happen if she tried to cross it.

She continued walking when she came to the back gate. Normally the gate would be closed with a guard not too far away watching it. He would release the lock so the gate would retract and when the guests or deliveries left, he would manually push the gate back into its locked position. But tonight, to Gwen's surprise, was different.

For the second time, in less than ten minutes, she was looking at an unlocked and unmanned doorway out of Pence. This time, the gate was wide open and there was no guard to be seen. First, she crept, then as she got closer to the gate and still seeing no one, she ran through it.

Gwen made her way through the cemetery that was in the back of the facility. Then down a mile long walk along a winding road. Finally, she reached a small strip mall at the bottom of the hill.

From a short distance she spotted a store clerk alone. He looked to either be cleaning up or preparing to close the store for the night. She wondered what she would say to him. She knew that it wouldn't be long before the patrolling guards inside Pence would find her room door broken and she had escaped. But what really troubled her was what was Blankenship going to do to her.

The door opened to the store and the bell that hung in front of it chimed.

"Hello.... we're closed. Hello..." The man said as he was in an aisle sweeping bits of garbage to be collected.

"Hullooooo....." Gwen said, sobbing. "I need some help! Is there someone here who could help me..."

"Hello?" The man leaned the broom against the shelf where some of the laundry detergents sat. *"Excuse me, Miss... is something wrong?"*

"Yeeessssss! Please help me! My boyfriend left me and I don't know where I'm at and I need to get to a place where I can get a bus home. I'm pregnant and I can't be out here late at night, the doctor's orders!"

"Oh! Oh...uhhhmm... I don't know--"

"PLEASE! YOU HAVE TO HELP ME, PLEASE!"

Gwen cried out. She held her head in her hands and cried even louder.

"Miss, please don't cry. It'll be alright. Let me see what I can do. I have to close the store but maybe I can drop you off somewhere close by and you could get a ride from there?"

"Could you?" Gwen said as she wiped her eyes with her sleeve. "I don't know how I got myself into this. I came here with my boyfriend and we went to visit his sister who's in that place not too far from here... what's it called?"

"Oh, you mean Pence prison?"

"Pence? That sounds like it but I'm not sure. Maybe, I don't know. All I know is that he told me to wait right here and he'd be right back and I didn't see him again and it's been a couple of hours now. I'm hungry and I'm tired."

"Oh, don't worry, Miss. I'll get you something to eat and I'll take you to where ever you need to go."

"It's not going to be too much trouble for you, is it sir?"

"No, miss. I'll just be a little late going home but my family will understand. Just wait right here for me. I'll go to lock up the back and I'll bring you some snacks for you to eat, okay."

"You're a blessing from God, you know that, right?"

"Thank you. I believe we were put here to help one another." He untied his apron and as he walked to the back, he turned to Gwen, *"I'll be right back!"*

"I'll be right here! God bless you!"

The store clerk talked about a shopping center not more than a half an hour away where there she could find a telephone booth to call a relative who could come to pick her up.

Gwen gave him a hug and waved to him as he turned his pickup truck around and headed back to Pence Springs. Gwen waited until she was out of sight before she walked some distance and sat on a bench.

Okay, how am I gonna get to Charleston before I get caught here? Gwen thought to herself. What will I do when I get there? How will I eat? Where can I get a job? Who will give me a job?

All of these questions began to trouble Gwen. Then the question she avoided acknowledging came to her awareness. What happens when I get caught and how much extra time would I have to serve for escaping?

Gwen walked around the mall then paced back and forth in one secluded area. She mulled over those questions and the consequences until she saw it was almost 11 p.m. One thing was clear to her at that moment: this mall was too close to Pence for the police not to stop and look for her here.

Gwen came around the front and saw a middle-aged, heavy-set man loading something in the back of his truck. He looked as if he was a stranger passing through and picking up some supplies from one of the stores in the mall. Gwen decided to see if her hunch was true.

"Excuse me, sir. I'm stranded and I was wondering if I could ask you a question."

The man looked at her and then pushed a huge log inside the bed of the truck.

"Yes, young lady. How can I help you?"

"Well, sir. My boyfriend's car broke down about a mile, a mile and a half from here and he has to get it towed and repaired before it can be used. I have to get back to Charleston tonight because as you could see, I'm pregnant and my mother's taking care of my other children. Do you think you could give me a ride as far as Charleston? If you're headed that way?"

The man stood up straight and looked Gwen up and down. He walked around her to get to the passenger side of the truck, but not before Gwen noticed that he was looking at her from behind. Gwen understood what that glance meant, if he were going to offer her a ride.

"Well, I'll tell ya what, Miss. This happens to be your lucky night. I've been here in town for a few days, visitin' my brother who doesn't live too far from here. I just stopped at this store right there to get some supplies for my store. Where'd you say you were goin' again?"

"Charleston, sir."

"Yes, Charleston. Well, I'm from a town just south of downtown, you might have heard of it if you're from Charleston, it's called Vandalia. Ever heard of it?"

"Yes, it sounds familiar but I've never been there."

"Good. I mean, good that I'm headed in the same area. Now, you'll just have to let me know where you want me to drop you off. Now, I'm just gonna move a few things around so you can sit up in the front seat without any problems."

Gwen saw the man reach in and quickly push things aside. He pulled a small box with papers haphazardly thrown inside and put inside the trunk. He walked back to the passenger side and helped Gwen inside.

Trapped Between Two Mountains

"You comfortable?"

"Yes. Thank you so much. I really appreciate it. I wish I had some money to pay for the trip but my purse is with my boyfriend in his car."

"Not to worry. Everything's already taken care of. I've got a full tank of gas and this truck is fitter than a bull with a belly full of green grass after a long summer shower."

Gwen shook her head and thanked him for the hand up into his truck.

Gwen guessed the trip from this mall to Charleston would be about 70 miles or so and at about the 60 miles per hour that he was driving, she figures she'd be in Charleston about 1 a.m. The man smiled at Gwen and would occasionally tap her on the leg.

"I never did get your name, Miss"

"Oh, I'm sorry, my name is Linda."

"Linda. Why that's a pretty name. Where are you from, Linda? If you don't mind me askin' cause you don't sound like no Charleston girl originally."

"No. Originally, I'm from Chicago. My parents moved to Charleston when I was a teenager and then I started to go to school down there. That's where I met my boyfriend."

The man slowly moved his hand in circles around Gwen's left knee.

"And, what about your boyfriend. What does he do?"
"Oh, my boyfriend's a business man. He has a business where he sets traps."

"Like a fisherman?"
"I guess, you could say that. He doesn't involve me too much in his business."

"I see. It seems to me like he should, a pretty thing like you could attract more business."
"You think so?"

"Yep, I sure do. I mean, you could attract lots of customers with just your looks and believe me, that's half the battle. But, once you get them in the door, the rest is up to you. Boy, I sure do wish I had someone like you working for me."

Gwen gently put her hand on top of his as he moved up her leg.

"Well, what kind of work would I be doing?"

The man tried to nudge his hand a little further up Gwen's leg but felt Gwen's hand resisting him. He put his hand back on the wheel and glanced at Gwen from his side eye.

"I don't know. It seems to me, like you could do almost anything you wanted to. I mean, heck, just having you around would bring more people around and you could charm them into buying more supplies and stuff. It could be a win for us all, if you'd consider it."

"Oh, I see. Well, how do I apply?"

The man smiled then looked at Gwen.

"Maybe we could stop by someplace and get something to eat, 'cause I know you're hungry and maybe see what kind of skill you have."

"Okay. That sounds interesting. But, isn't your wife expecting you home as soon as possible?"

"Naw, she knows that I git in when I git in. She knows that there's a lot of traffic and bad weather along the way."

"Okay. I know somewhere we can talk about it on Court Street."

"Great. I think things'll work out just fine. Just fine."

The truck turned onto Court Street about 1:35 a.m. Gwen pointed to a hotel near The Last Chance Club and told him to park in the open space.

"Let me see if they have a room open so we can talk."

Gwen ran through the door and spoke with a girl she had known for some time. The girl was surprised to see Gwen but when Gwen promised to explain everything later, the girl knew that Gwen was about to scam the guy following her in.

Gwen waited off to the side as the girl behind the counter and the gentleman spoke. Gwen put up two fingers to the girl as the man pulled out his wallet and handed her some bills. The girl handed the man a key and told him that check out was 10 a,m.

"Well, let's go, Linda. We have a lot to talk about."
"Jim, wait just a minute. Go upstairs, I'll meet you there in five minutes. I'm going next door to get us something to eat. Do you have a couple of extra dollars for a fish and chips meal?"
"I suppose I do."

The man took out his wallet and handed Gwen a couple of bills, but before he could put his wallet back, Gwen smiled and pulled out another bill from out of his wallet.

"That's just in case, it went up!"
"Okay, now, Linda you're getting kinda expensive here. Be back soon, I'll be ready."
"Okay, not more than ten minutes, fifteen if there's a line."

The man waved Gwen off and walked took the stairs to their room. Gwen walked over to the counter and whispered something in the counter girl's ear.

Gwen bought a can of soda from The Last Chance and walked across the street from the hotel. She heard the sirens sound and two police cars stop in front of the hotel. As she stood in the shadows of a building across the street, she witnessed the police walking the man into their squad car. He looked to be shouting something at the officers before they bent his head down and pushed him in the backseat. Both police cars drove off. Gwen walked back into the hotel and walked out with half of the money the driver paid to the counter girl.

It was very late and Gwen walked a few blocks, missing her old life but worrying about the present and the future one. She thought about Jink, she thought about their child and she thought about being on the run. This wasn't the safe, stable life she planned for herself but she didn't know what else to do.

She thought about calling her friend, Magistrate Carol Foute, but then she realized that she would be compromising Carol's position if it were known that she was talking with a fugitive. She couldn't call her mother, Lila Mae, because she didn't want to worry her. The only person left to call was her father. Gwen held out no hope that he would be supportive, but she still dropped a dime in the telephone coin slot.

"Hello, Daddy, it's me, Gwen."

"Gwen, I've been worried sick about you. Where are you?"

"You've been worried sick about me? What do you mean?"

"Don't play dumb with me. You forgot that I have a police scanner here at home? I know all about you escaping from prison. You have to go back!"

"I know. Can I explain?"

"Explain, what? That you broke out of prison and that you're considered dangerous? Do you know how that makes me look?"

Trapped Between Two Mountains

"This is not your problem. You didn't even ask me why I left."

"Well, why did you leave?"

"Nevermind. I'll figure it out myself."

"Gwen! Wait. Do yourself a favor and turn yourself in. Call the agency and tell them where you are and that you made a mistake. They might have leniency on you."

"That's the best you can do?"

"What more do you want me to do?"

"Okay, thanks. Bye."

Gwen hung up the phone and walked around Court Street. Occasionally she'd look up and see police cars driving by but none seemed as if they were looking for a fugitive. Gwen also noticed the driver's truck *was* gone when she went back a few hours later. She looked in her pocket and saw almost forty dollars in different denominations crumpled in her back pocket. She realized that it would only cover a day or two before it ran out. She knew her dad was right and that for her own safety, she needed to resolve the Pence issue as quickly as possible.

She walked back to the phone booth by the Greyhound bus station and dialed the State's Correctional Office. After she identified herself, she promised that she'd wait right there and they, in turn, promised that no harm would come to her and that she'd get a fair hearing.

Within fifteen minutes two squad cars pulled up to the bus station with four officers coming out. Gwen sat in a restaurant across the street looking out. She looked at the officers scouring the area and talking on their phones. She was terrified at the scene that she knew was all about her. For the first time in several days, she was terrified to even move an inch.

Gwen lifted up the menu and looked at something else to order.

"Can I help you, ma'am?"

A waitress asked from the other side of the table.

"Ahh, yes! I'll have a plate of scrambled eggs, two sausage links and a cup of coffee."
"Would you like a piece of cake with that, as well?"
"Yes! Yes, that would be nice."
"Will there be anything else?"
"No, thank you. I'm just killing time."

Gwen finished her breakfast about an hour after both police cars had left the scene. She wondered what would happen to her now, knowing that the Charleston Police was officially on the lookout for her. Gwen spent a night in a hotel then walked back to the phone booth.

This time when she called, she asked to speak directly with the commissioner. To her surprise, the officer on the other end of the line gave Gwen the commissioner's home phone number.

"Hello."

"Good morning, Commissioner?"

"Yes, who's speaking?"

"My name is Gwen Collins."

"Collins... COLLINS! Yes, yes. Where are you dear?"

"I'm here in Charleston. I want to turn myself in."

"Okay, Miss Collins. We had some officers come to pick you up yesterday. Why didn't you stay where you were?"

"I got scared. That's why I'm calling you because I wanted to at least speak with someone with authority."

"Okay, I'm listening."

"First of all, I'm pregnant and I'm gonna have my baby in a few weeks."

"Oh, dear! They didn't tell me that."

"And, I need to tell you about the conditions at Pence."

"What about Pence? Isn't Blankenship treating the women fairly?"

"Not really, sir. We can't make calls. She won't allow us to receive mail from our loved ones, even when we know mail has come. She creates a hostile environment by using her guards to talk down to us and a whole lot of other things. And, I almost forgot, she doesn't allow all of us who want to attend church services to go when they have it. She likes to have these boring knitting classes. I grew up in church and that's where I feel most at home."

"She discourages you from going to church? That's interesting." The police commissioner didn't say anything for a

second. "I tell you what, what if I came down to Charleston and picked you up personally, would you allow me to do that? I promise nothing will happen to you when you get back to Pence and you'll be safe."

"Yes, sir."

"Okay, good. I'll pick you up in my car. It's this model car, I'm this height and I'll be wearing this. You'll also see my state-issued police tag around my license plate. You can have Thanksgiving dinner with us tonight and then I'll have some officers take you back to Pence. Does that sound alright with you."

"Yes, sir. I'll be here. I don't have any baggage. I'll be sitting in the restaurant half a block away from the bus station. So, when I see your car I'll come out."

"Do I have your word."

"Yes, sir, you have my word. My dad works in law enforcement and he was the one that told me to contact you and turn myself in."

"Very good. Your father's a good man. I'll be over as soon as I can, we're probably talking about forty minutes or so."

"I'll be here waiting."

"See you then."

Gwen had dinner with the Commissioner and his wife. They had Cornish hen along with macaroni and cheese, rice, candied yam, corn, freshly baked muffins and some soft drinks.

The commissioner sat Gwen down and told her about the severity of her crime. He promised not to move Gwen from the minimum- security facility but he couldn't promise that there wouldn't be any recrimination from Blankenship. However, he assured her that if anything happened she could call him and they'd work through the situation.

After two hours, the commissioner and his wife thanked Gwen for her honesty and shook her hands. Two policemen came to the commissioner's door and took Gwen away in their car back to Pence Springs. Gwen waved to the commissioner and he waved back.

Gwen walked into Pence and found Blankenship waiting in the hallway, silently staring at her. Two of Pence's officers signed the release papers from the commissioner's officers. They walked upstairs to the first floor of rooms for the inmates only to walk past them to a long but narrowing path that led to a long steel door. A red steel door with no window.

  One of the officers lifted the bundle of keys from her waist and withdrew a long, thick keys that was unlike any of the other keys on her ring. The officer used both of there hands to turn the lock until the screech of the bolt loosened the door for the other officer to pull it open. They stood back and looked at Gwen. Gwen moved slowly; the dark doorway hid the contents of the room she'd now call home until Blankenship was appeased.

Once inside, she saw a small frame and a thin mattress across from her. There were no books or magazines. No pictures, tv or a radio. Nothing in a room that was half the size of the one she was assigned to, nothing except a steel commode and a tiny window just above the steel basin. It would be eighty-eight days before she'd return to her original room.

Last night seemed like a half hour ago but it was the next morning.

She didn't sleep well having gotten up every few hours just to be certain there were no ghosts standing by the head of her bed. At least, if it were daylight, the sun would reveal their true nature.

Her mind settled as she rubbed her eyes trying to clear it from the weight of everything that happened. Her mind went from the fear of the warden to the screaming inmate to the personal hook-ups that happened all around her. She had no one to relate to in Pence.

She heard the wake-up call. Gwen nodded to herself just before she splashed water all over her face. Her eyes were now closed to prevent soap from entering. She cupped her hands together and splashed her face again. The cold water was like a hot cup of coffee.

It took just a few minutes but she was dressed to meet the day. It took a while but she started making friends on her own. She was largely hidden behind the good vibes that Donna had created. She also detected very quickly that being friendly and assertive was met with suspicion and mistrust especially when she made small talk with the guards.

She noticed the stone-faced silence and non-verbal commands. Everyone had a place and everyone understood this. This was when it dawned on her that she inadvertently violated one of Pence's unwritten rules.

How was she to start a conversation? She looked around the room as different thoughts came in and out of her head. She heard a noise behind her and when she turned to take a look, she mistakenly pushed her chair into Miss Valerie. Valerie's tray jiggled as she caught her step. Gwen put both hands to her mouth but before she could apologize, Valerie looked at her with an annoyed gaze.

"I know it's an accident, but be careful. Don't let it happen again." With that, Valerie walked off and sat by herself at the corner table. She grumbled a few words to herself not loud enough for anyone else to discern, but the expression on her face and the movement of her lips left nothing in doubt.

As Gwen watched this, she felt a tap on her right shoulder. It was one of the guards.

"Collins, you have got to know where you're place is at," she said as she wrote something down on her notepad.
"Am I being written up?" Gwen asked, excitedly.
"Yep!"
"Why, it was an accident. I didn't do it on purpose."
"Collins, relax! This is just routine. We keep a log of everything that we see in case something happens, we know exactly how it came about."

The guard turned around and walked back to her place by the entrance doorway. Gwen shook her head and looked back in the direction of Vonda who was just staring down at her plate as she ate.

*** *** ***

The racial demographics at Pence was about fifty percent white and fifty percent black with roughly half of each group under thirty and the other half over thirty (but less than forty.) There were no women over fifty years old at Pence.

Valerie was one of the few women in Pence serving time for murder. Besides Valerie, Pence had three other women serving time for murder: Vivian, Elda and Dolly. They were respected by the other inmates because of their crimes and they were given space to be by themselves by the guards. The average sentence given to women for murder was five to eighteen years, but Valerie was convicted of killing her husband and her sentence was life.

Donna couldn't guarantee that she got all of Vivian's details right but she told Gwen that Valerie lived with her alcoholic husband and teenage daughters on the outskirts of Charleston in one of the affluent suburbs. Valerie played her part as the dutiful housewife and mother. She gave up a promising career as an artist and a model when she met the manager of an insurance company after one of her performances. He convinced her to postpone her career until after they started a family.

Years went by and after giving birth to two girls, Valerie approached her husband with her desire to resume her career after the girls were old enough to go to school by themselves. Soft talk about a not-too-distant future turned to elevated voices about age and weight to drunken bouts and accusations of infidelity. Valerie's girls would often find Valerie crying on her bed with bruise marks around her eyes and throat. Valerie considered divorce, but the good, pastoral advice she received from church exhorted her to honor and obey her husband's wishes; because after all, the man is the head of the household.

The insurance company that her husband worked for was sold to its main competitor and Valerie's husband didn't fit with the company's new plans. After seventeen years, Valerie's husband was unemployed and unemployable. He was unable to hold a steady job and his excessive drinking became more frequent.

Trapped Between Two Mountains

One afternoon after shopping at a consignment store, Valerie returned home. She called to her husband while she dropped the bag with the clothes on the living room couch. She put the small grocery bag on the kitchen counter. She looked at her watch and realized that her daughters should have been home. Her calls to her daughters went unanswered.

She left the kitchen and took off her shoes, putting them aside and approached their bedroom door.

She was about to ask why the dishes were not washed, but as she turned the knob, the bedroom door opened to the sight of Valerie's husband and their daughters.

Valerie later told the judge that she had no recollection of what actually happened afterward except she found herself in her bedroom holding one of her husband's guns and him laying naked on the floor in the doorway.

*** *** ***

There was a knock on Blankenship's door. The guard, Mrs. Crawford, a rotund woman who always wore navy blue double knit, polyester pants, knocked again. As she slowly opened the door she saw Blankenship rocking in her chair talking on the phone while looking out the window. Blankenship, whose blazer was draped around her chair, had her back to the door.

Blankenship finished her thought and turned around to see Officer Crawford holding the daily prisoner reports for her. Blankenship motioned for Crawford to wait she'd be off in a minute. She resumed her conversation before telling the caller that she'd have to call her back later. Blankenship said nothing to Crawford as she received the stack from her. Crawford was about to turn to leave when Blankenship tipped her glasses down her nose bridge while thumbing through the stack;

"Anything going on that I need to know about, Crawford?"

Crawford turned towards Blankenship,

"Nothing. All of the women were on time for their duties, came to lunch on time and kept the chatter to a reasonable level."

"That's good to hear. The board has been wanting to know how we've managed to keep the women in line. They're questioning if we're running a tight ship since we haven't been submitting any behavioral reports back to them. We're either hiding or condoning bad behavior."

"The women have been behaving. I have nothing to report other than a small incident with one of the newer inmates. Oh, I forgot her name... oh! Collins! That's it, Collins. Collins had accidentally bumped into Valerie."

"Was it serious?"

"No. She apologized to Vonda and sat back down to the table without incident."

Blankenship tapped the stack of papers on her desk evening out the sides, then placed the stack in a different direction for the stack below it.

"How is Collins coming along? Isn't that the short, black one who used to associate with Donna... what's her last name, again?"

"Yes, Warden, she's the one. She's the same one. She seems friendly and says good things to everyone she sees. And, she is very respectful to the guards. We've had no complaints about her. The other inmates and I were talking about the black ones don't necessarily like her. She's from out of state and these local girls don't trust strangers."

"Oh, really? Well, that's interesting." Blankenship peered through Crawford for a second while tapping a pencil on her desk. *"I want you to keep a close eye on Collins. She may be useful to us. We have about..."*

Blankenship turned to the other side of her desk and pulled out a stacked folder with a bunch of photographs sticking out. She flipped through the stack then put the folder down on the desk in front of her.

"I have about a dozen more women the state is sending here from Charleston... no serious criminals... prostitutes, drug users, that sort of thing, but it would be good to know what's going on with them at all times. I don't want Pence to be some kind of girl-scout sleepover. Maybe we can have Collins be our ears? What do you think?"

"I... I don't know. How would we do that?" Crawford looked shocked.

"Simple. I want you to treat Collins differently, but within limits. And I want you to tell the other guards to encourage and befriend Collins; this way, Collins will feel as if she has some credit with the guards because of her personality. Every so often, I want each of you to strike up a conversation with her and let her tell us about what the other inmates are doing. The thing is, I want Collins to think that the guards are her friends."

"I see," Crawford said. "I see."

"Well, lookey here, lookey here! Ain't this somethin'! Little Miss Cheerful wants to play cards!"

Dorothy said in a mocking tone and looking up to Gwen from her seat at the table. Gwen looked around the table and recognized a few new faces who just arrived from Charleston, but were already seated at the good table to play cards. How did that happen, Gwen thought to herself. She was surprised to see Miss D. amongst the ranks. She hadn't seen her since she was arraigned almost a year ago.

Gwen noticed that few of the women took notice of her being there. It was to Gwen a signal that they'd rather not associate with her personally. This bewildered Gwen because just fourteen months before she'd be hanging out in the same places as many of these women. She could place where every one of them sat in Candyman's. It took Gwen a whole week to raise up enough courage to ask to play with them and now this was their answer? It didn't make sense. Dorothy's words were still in the air when Gwen thought to herself, she could turn around and make a place for herself with other people or she could fight to be accepted. The seconds to make that decision was rapidly disappearing.

"*Well, let me tell you Miss Sunshine, this ain't no place for training bras!*" Dorothy said as she juggled a cigarette in her mouth and playing a hand in Spades. "*Why don't you just sit yourself down and watch a soap opera or go down to one of Blankenship's crochet classes?*"

Gwen felt her blood starting to boil, her head felt light and her breath, heavier.

"I'll have you to know, I don't normally play with women because they have no balls. I play with the boys because they can hang with me."

"*Oh! Ohhhh, so you think you got game, huh?*"

"I ain't no punk. Just ask my boyfriend." Gwen said as she put her hands on her waist.

Dorothy leaned back in her chair and exhaled a cloud of smoke from the side of her mouth.

"I like you, Collins. I must admit, I didn't think I would, but, I like you. You got spunk. I got a question for you. You think you can play Prison Spades?"

"Prison Spades? What's that?"

"Yeah, Prison Spades. Prison Spades is Spades doing time. That's where we play for long odds. Sometimes it lasts weeks, sometimes months. You see all of my girls here..." Dorothy said, pointing to the women around the table and those standing around the players. "This is my crew. We rep the Second Floor and if you're gonna play with us, you gotta prove yourself against them before you can sit at this table."

Dorothy turned to her right and nodded her head to a tall, slim girl with thin eyebrows, thin lips and corn-rows. She, in turn, went into her pocket and produced a pack of cigarettes. With a flick of her hand, a single cigarette slid from the bunch. She lit it and handed it to Dorothy. Dorothy took the cigarette and inhaled one long drag. In the midst of exhaling, she looked at Gwen and handed her the cigarette.

"So, small fry, what you gotta say?"

Gwen slowly took the cigarette from Dorothy and took a drag. She looked down and exhaled. She handed the cigarette back to Dorothy and for a moment she froze; she wondered was this acceptance more than just wanting to play cards and to have some friends to talk to. She didn't really know, so she looked back at Dorothy, who was now staring at her while cracking a smile.

"Okay, I'm in."

"Good! That what I expected. You gotta be tough and you can't be intimidated cause people will take advantage of you."

Gwen nodded without saying a word. Dorothy held the cigarette to her lips and slowly took another pull.

"Two more things you gotta understand. One, we play to win. There ain't no draw's and there certainly ain't no losing. And two, everything you see is on the down-low. You don't see nothing, know nothing and hear nothing. Got it?"

"Yeah, I got it."

Just as Gwen finished answering, she felt a tap on her shoulder. She turned around and saw a familiar face.

"Heyyyyyyy!"

Gwen leaned in to give Wilhemina a hug, but Wilhemena pushed Gwen's arm away.

"I hope this boyfriend you're talking about is not Jink."

"Hey, it's great to see you. How's everyone back home? Have you heard from Jink-"

"I said, I hope you're not referring to Jink," Wilhemina solemnly said.

"I.. I.. well, have you heard from him? I haven't gotten anything from him but a card and that was more than three months ago, but he didn't say anything."

"I don't know where he is, but that doesn't concern you. Don't concern yourself with my husband. Why haven't you got that through your thick skull?"

"Wilhemina, wait! Wait a minute! I didn't start the relationship, he did. As a matter of fact, when I asked you if you were married to him, you told me, no. You told me, Jink was your brother. So you had a hand in our relationship."

"Listen, you! Any fool could've seen we were together. You just pretended as if you didn't know."

Gwen took a step back and crossed her arms.

"Oh, no you didn't! You didn't just call me a fool! What woman in her right mind would give her husband to another woman? That tells me that you don't have what it takes to keep a man satisfied."

Terri took a step forward and looked at Gwen,

"You say that again and I'll smack the taste out of your mouth."
"I'd like to see you try it," Gwen said as she stepped out of her heels.

Trapped Between Two Mountains

Two guards grabbed both women. The normally loud second floor recreation room was now whisper-quiet save Gwen, Wilhemena, Terri and the two guards.

Each of the guards wrote down the names of the women and jotted down their personal complaints. Gwen talked over Wilhemena and Terri telling the guard that she doesn't allow anyone to talk crazy to her. Wilhemina, told her guard that Gwen was a home wrecker and was keeping a relationship with her husband behind bars. All of the women were immediately sent back to their rooms for the rest of the night.

**** ***

When Officers Ward and Crawford approached Warden Blankenship's office, they noticed the door slightly ajar. The two looked at each other but instead of outright knocking, they both took a step back and leaned in to hear what Blankenship was talking about.

"Yeah, that's right. I can't wait. I'm looking forward to it. Yes... yes...it would be my heart's desire to know that you're going to be there, even if it's just a few sections away. I can't stop thinking of you. Wouldn't it be delightful to hear Lotte perform some of Kurt's compositions? Splendid.... I can't wait. Yes, yes. Good night to you too, my love." After the two guards heard the sound of the receiver placed on the base, a voice from inside the office spoke up: *"You, two, may come in now."*

The guards looked at each other then slowly pushed the door open before coming in.

"Don't you know it's rude to eavesdrop on someone's conversation?"

Blankenship said as she sat in her chair facing them. But neither of them said anything. One of the guards handed Blankenship the daily prison reports,

"Anything unusual happened today before I read the reports?"

"Well, Warden Blankenship..." Ward said, "We did have an exchange between two inmates over a man earlier today."

"A man! Why in the world would they fight over a man? Is he here on the premises?"

"No, warden, a civilian in Charleston. Supposedly one of the inmates is married to a guy who's having an affair with another inmate here, and they both admit knowing about each other."

"Well, who are they?"

"Inmate Collins, Inmate Wilhelmina Jones and Inmate Terri.... I forgot her last name," Ward said.

"You mean Jones is cheating with Collin's husband?"

"No warden, it's the other way around!"

"Collins is cheating with Jones' husband...and, they both know it?"

"Yes, warden. Apparently, Jones wants Collins to stop speaking with her husband who she admitted to setting up with Collins and a few other women. The third woman, Terri, was defending Jones. She's also a part of the Charleston group. She got involved and got into a scuffle with Collins and Collins bit her finger."

"Oh, no! This is not good. I don't want the State knowing that we could have a potential problem with inmates and spouses and lovers all under the same roof. But, I also don't want to involve Pence in a domestic issue that has nothing to do with them being here."

"I have an idea, warden," Crawford interrupted.

"Well, what is it?"

"Collins was pregnant with Jones' husband's baby. That's the baby she gave to her mother to take care of until she's released. Terri knows Jones' husband but feels that Collins took advantage of him. So, if we eliminated the correspondence from the guy to the women here, then all of the women would think that he is a lowlife that abandoned them. They'll be forced to be civil to each other because they are all they have."

Blankenship stared at her for a second and slowly said,

"That's a good idea! That's a very good idea! Did any of you write them up?"

"Yes, we wrote all of them up," Ward said. "It's right there in our reports."

"Good! Very good! We have some additional leverage on Collins because she'll feel grateful to us for leniency. I'll deal with Collins in a few days... I have her right where I want her."

"MAIL CALL...... MAIL CALL!"

The voice of the officer reverberated from the downstairs lobby. In truth, no one needed to hear it a second time. After the first announcement, everyone could hear the immediate rumblings in each of the rooms if one were to walk through the halls.

Mail Call was the second most exciting thing you could hear next to Visitation Time (of course, with the notable exception of Meal Time.) Mail Call felt a little bit like Christmas morning. It was a time where an inmate's loved ones showed tangible acts of kindness, where the gifts and cash were always expected and appreciated. Letters, postcards and packages of all stripes were indeed the outside world saying, "Hello!"

Within a few minutes, Gwen found herself in the middle of the cue. Some walked past her with a few letters, some had packages, some had both and some were sullen with their arms to their sides. At the sight of those women who left empty-handed, Gwen thought to herself in that moment, It's gonna be alright, you'll be out soon! Gwen walked up to the counter and the attending officer looked at the clipboard of names.

"Next! "Collins. C-O-L-L-I-N-S."

"Okay, we have quite a few things for you today. We also have a notice that you have to see the warden right after you sign for your things."

"Warden Blankenship? Why?"

"I don't know why. This is my job to follow orders. She left a note that she needed to see you and I suggest that you stop asking so many questions and holding up the line."

Gwen signed for her mail, including a medium sized box.

The excitement of carrying all of those things past the other women waiting in line was tempered by a small detour she needed to take to get to Blankenship's door. There, Gwen stood with a few letters and a box in front of a door with a placard that read: Velma Blankenship, Warden. Office of the State of West Virginia.

Knock. Knock.

"*Come in,*" Blankenship said as she repositioned herself from the officer who was sitting in one of the two armchairs on the other side of Blankenship's desk.

As Gwen open the door, she pushed it with her foot as she was still juggling the mail she had with a partially free hand to turn the knob. Neither Blankenship nor Officer Crawford budged from their seats to help Gwen.

"*Inmate Collins... I'm glad you're here. Please take the seat next to the officer. You can either rest your stuff here the on the end of the desk nearest to you or you can put them on the floor.*"

Blankenship tipped her glasses down her nose bridge and looked at Gwen over the top of her frame.

"*I was just telling Officer Crawford that we need more volunteers to join the dance class. Do you think you might be interested?*"

"Oh...mmm... I.... I'm not...sure... but I think I'll eventually say yes."

"Great. That's very good."

Blankenship pushed her chair back, opened the front drawer of her desk and pulled out a letter.

"*Collins, I'm holding a letter that's addressed to you but it has come to my attention that the sender is not someone you're supposed to be dealing with.*"

Trapped Between Two Mountains

Gwen sat there silently. She felt the strange feeling of fear growing inside of her.

"Collins, I'm getting very concerned about you. It seems like every other day I'm getting some report about you. Now, I hear that you're fighting with Wilhemina Jones over a man?"

"No Warden Blankenship, let me explain. I thought he was single. He approached me. When I told him that I didn't want a relationship because I wanted to concentrate on my work at the Job Corp, he refused to leave me alone."

"You mean, he pretended he wasn't married."

"Yes."

"So where does Wilhemina come into this?"

"People started telling me that he was married. I couldn't understand why they were saying that. He was with me all the time except when I was in the Job Corp building."

"Wilhemina....."

"People told me it was her, but, I wouldn't see her around him alone. She was always with some of the other women who worked for Jink. When I confronted Jink about the rumors, he said let's go and find out for yourself. So, we found Wilhemina a few blocks away and she was standing outside the bar for some reason and he asked her to come over and talk with us for a second. He told her that I had a question to ask her."

"So what happened?"

"I said to her, 'are you and Jink together, like married....'" Gwen began to get fidgety as she started to bite her nails. "She told me that she was his sister."

"His sister!"
"Yes, his sister."

Blankenship took a deep, deep breath and leaned into Gwen.

"Collins... Collins, you need to get yourself away from lowlife people. I can't imagine that your family would approve of what you're doing."

Gwen stared at Blankenship with the thought of the insult still resounding in her mind.

"In any case, I need to inform you that I am obligated to maintain order for this place. I also need to inform you starting immediately, I have removed Jink from your Approved Correspondence List. You no longer qualify to receive any correspondence from him, nor are you to send any correspondence to him."
"Why! I didn't do anything!"

Gwen stood up looking at Blankenship.

"Sit Down. Collins.... don't forget to whom you are speaking to," Blankenship said, as she stood up from her chair. "Inmate Collins, did you not just hear me? I said, they'll be no more contact with Wilhelmina's husband for the remainder of your stay here."

Both women stared at each other for a second. Gwen didn't notice that Officer Crawford was standing guard between them during the heated conversation. Crawford looked toward Blankenship.

"Warden Blankenship, should I escort the inmate back to her room?"

Blankenship looked at Crawford, then to Gwen,

"Collins, that'll be all for right now. From now on, I will personally be monitoring all the mail that comes to Pence with your name on it."

Gwen sat on the floor next to her bed and sobbed for awhile. She threw everything on the floor including her box. She laid on her bed and looked at the cracks on the ceiling hoping that any crack would lead her to something pleasant. She imagined they were a secret code that would lead the seeker out of Pence. After a few minutes, she sat up and saw her mail scattered all over the place. She picked up two letters and took the box and placed it on her bed closest to the wall.

The first letter she opened was from her father. Inside the envelope was a folded piece of paper Written on it was the message, "I deposited twenty dollars in your commissary account. Stay well and get a good night's rest. Love, Dad."

Gwen put the paper on the side of her bed and ripped up the envelope that contained her father's note.

Gwen opened the second letter, it was from her mother, Lila Mae. Even though Gwen told her mother she was okay and not to send her any money, Lila Mae still managed to send ten dollars to her commissary account as well.

The message from Lila Mae was the same as it always was, *"I love you. Stay strong. The Lord will guide you and see you through this. The family is okay and your brothers and sisters miss you very much. You always have a place to come home to. You're still my baby, no matter what. Love, mom."*

Gwen held the letter close to her heart and closed her eyes as tears streamed down her face. Every time she received a letter from her mother, she knew two things were about to be revealed: one, her mother was going to send money even though she couldn't afford it. Gwen knew she most likely had to sacrifice a meal or two for her to be able to send some commissary money. And two, despite the mistakes she made, Lila Mae loved her unconditionally and would always stand up for her. Gwen always found herself crying after reading Lila Mae's letters because she felt as if she let her mother down.

Gwen got up and crawled back into bed. She held the two bills in her hands for a second then put them back down. She reached over and pulled the box to her lap. She looked at the box and looked at the handwriting wondering for a moment who could it be. It looked familiar but it was definitely from a woman. She saw it was from Kentucky and deduced that it could only be from her favorite aunt.

She opened the box and there were several, double-sided, handwritten pages on top of a smaller box. Gwen lifted up the smaller box and discovered it was a carton of her favorite, Kool Filtered Kings Cigarettes.

"Aunt Gladys," Gwen spoke to herself, "You're the best!"

Gwen quickly grabbed a pack from the carton and opened it to withdraw a cigarette. She lit one, inhaled, then closed her eyes and slowly exhaled. This brand, the flavor and the sensation reminded Gwen of contented moments in Madisonville and in Charleston.

She took another puff and exhaled quickly as she picked up the stack of papers that Grand-Aunt Gladys wrote.

"Gwendolyn Faye! My favorite niece! How are you? I hope you're hanging in there. I just left your mother's new place and she told me that she just posted a letter to you.

I know it's been awhile and I know the last time I heard from you, you wanted to know how everyone's been doing. I had been thinking about what I would say to you but feeling worried how you'd take it. The other part of me says I need to tell you because you're grown now and hopefully when you get out, you'll come home and be with us. Everyone misses you, your mother and your brothers and sisters miss you terribly.

"So, since I know that your mother (my niece) probably hasn't told you about life in Madisonville since you left, I am going to let you know about what's been going on here since you can think about how you want to deal with it instead of being surprised and shocked.

So, I'm going to start with the fact that we just came back from court. Me and Lila Mae and your brothers except for Michael (he's been away in college. I heard that he's working on his Master's degree in something) and your sisters. (I've got to tell you this before you read it in the newspaper): LeRoy (you remember LeRoy, your mother's boyfriend?) well, he was just sentenced to eight years in prison for murdering a friend of his from the coal mines in your mother's house. Phyllis saw the whole thing and she was in the newspaper as the state's witness.

Now, before you get scared and everything. She's alright. She was strong and her baby is okay. Oh! Did I tell you that your baby sister had a beautiful baby boy? He's so cute. Well, I'll talk to you about that at another time. I'm gonna try to tell you exactly what happened from the beginning, so you better be sitting down for this...."

Trapped Between Two Mountains

Gwen turned the page over to read from the top. She knew she needed to get herself prepared because if her mother kept a secret, certainly it was nothing pleasant to relate. She took a deep breath and heard her Aunt Gladys' voice in her head as she continued to read.

"Gwen, now stay with me child and remember what I just told you about you being grown up. Okay, here we go.
I got a call one night right after I came home from shopping. I had to stop and pick up some groceries but I couldn't get a taxi to drop me home, so I had five bags of grocery I had to carry. I had to make that long walk down the hill from that store. Anyway, just as I was coming in the house, the phone started ringing. As you can imagine I was in no mood for a long

conversation. I wasn't gonna answer it, but something didn't seem right to me. So anyway I picked up the phone. Somebody on the other end was screaming and crying. I didn't know who it was at first. After, I found out it was Phyllis. I asked her to calm down. I couldn't make heads or tails about what she was saying so I told her to 'Calm down! I'm coming right over!' I put on my slippers but I could hardly stand up, child. My feet were so sore and swollen (I was upset with myself because I forgot to buy that Dr. Scholl's and I just left the store.)

I walked as fast as I could, but you know my bunions been acting up on me. Oh, I forgot to mention this, if Lila Mae didn't tell you, she moved the family a few block away. She believed that lowlife Leroy and got into some financial trouble with the bank and the bank made Lila Mae give them your grandmother Cecil's house, but that's another story. Anyway, it took me about fifteen minutes to get over there. When I got there! Lord! When I got there, I heard that girl and that baby screaming and kicking up a fuss. I thought to myself, 'I should have taken two aspirin before I came over for my migraines'. So, I walked up to the doorway and I found the door open. I thought at first that one of your brothers and sisters had left it open because I just saw them down the street playing with some of the neighbor's kids. (And, I knew it was them cause they were wearing the same clothes that I saw them wearing just last weekend. It's only cause their momma's was away, cause she wouldn't have them in those same dirty clothes.)

"So, as I was pulling the door open, I called Phyllis' name to let her know it was me and I was coming in. Oh... my... god..., I'll *never forget what I saw when I walked in for the rest of my life..."*

*** *** ***

It was a calm summer afternoon about four o'clock. The days had been getting longer, but the extra daylight hours was an invitation to do things the nighttime commute prohibited. Some people found themselves staying in the city to either try the new Indian restaurant, catch a movie or a drink and or a dance at a juke joint. Small children played in abandoned homes boys made forts in makeshift clubhouses in nearby woods, while some girls braided each other's hair and others played jack-stones. Grandparents brought out trays of lemonade to watch the festivities from their rocking chairs.

Life was simple in Madisonville in the late nineteen sixties. There were few, if any, disturbances except for the occasional skirmishes in front of bars or in cars with people yelling racial obscenities.

Nothing was out of the ordinary at Lila Mae's new house. A few days earlier, Lila Mae received a letter informing her that her father was very ill. She left soon after for Indianapolis. She left Phyllis, the eldest of her children still living at home, to look after her younger siblings. Phyllis, almost twelve and a half as she'd say, was at home.

Phyllis was sitting on the living-room couch nursing her newborn son when she realized she could supplement her hungry, feeding son with a bottle of formula. She carefully got up from the couch and walked him to Lila Mae's bedroom where his crib was. She held him close and patted his back while gently rocking him. When she noticed his eyes were closed, she softly put him down and pulled the baby blanket over him.

Just then, she heard the creaking of the front door and the sound of footsteps running through the house. She turned back to the crib and saw her son falling asleep with his thumb in his mouth.

She walked quickly out of the room to see her younger brother and sister running in and out of the kitchen.

"Y'all stay outside now! I don't want you waking up the baby! Ain't none of y'all helping me to put him to sleep! Y'all stay outside 'til it's dark."

There was no response to her command except the creaking sound of the front door opening and closing. Phyllis walked quickly to the screened door.

"Y'all hear me? Don't come back 'til it's dark!"

From a distance she heard them respond, *"Okay!"* Then the muffled sound of small feet pattering down the road slowly dissipated in the distance. Phyllis walked back to the kitchen and put some water in a small saucepan. She placed a small baby bottle with formula inside before she heard the front door open again.

Only a few minutes passed when Phyllis heard the creak of the front door open again. Phyllis was about to yell to her brothers and sisters to keep it down but she was stopped by the heavy sound of the steps that came in. She waited for a second and asked,

"Hello?"
"Lila Mae, it's me! "
"No, it's me Phyllis! Come in"

Phyllis shook a little bit of formula onto the back of her hand, then tasted it. She put it back in the pan to warm. Leroy stuck his head in the kitchen doorway and said,

"Phyllis, where's your mother?"
"She ain't here. She went to see my granddad in Indianapolis. She'll be back on Thursday."
"Oh! Okay, well... me and my friend, Eddie, we gonna sit down right here and relax for a few minutes then we're gonna get up on outta here. You good with dat?"

Phyllis shrugged her shoulders,

"I guess." Phyllis wiped her moist hands on her shorts, *"Your friend wants some water cause we ain't got nothing else to drink."*

Leroy turned away from Phyllis,

Trapped Between Two Mountains

"Eddie... Eddie... you want some water?" Leroy walked away from the kitchen.

Then Phyllis heard Leroy say,

"Nah! He's alright. I'll get some later. Let's get this game going!"

Leroy walked back to the living-room and sat on the couch facing Eddie. As Phyllis peeked out of the kitchen doorway to see what was going on, she just saw both men sitting on the couch behind the coffee table. Too much extra. This detail crossed out is not needed. Leroy and Eddie moved the table to the side. Eddie shook his wrist vigorously, then lifting his hand over his head he followed through with a drop. His hand released two ivory- colored dice, which came to a stop by one of the table's legs.

Eddie jumped up and screamed out "YEAH!"

Leroy, who was still stooped over the dice reached for the small pile of bills that were on the floor between the two men but closer to the couch.

"Leroy, give me my money!"
"No! It's my money!"
"NO! I WON!"

Phyllis came running out of the kitchen and stood in front of the two men.

Trapped Between Two Mountains

"Y'all gotta stop all this shouting cause you're gonna wake my baby!" She said with her hands outstretched toward them.

In the moment that the men heard Phyllis' plea, Eddie reached over and grabbed the bills that were still in Leroy's hand and shoved it into his pocket. Leroy feeling the money leave his hands, ran around the table and swung at Eddie catching him on the chin.

The force of Leroy's punch and the imbalance of Eddie trying to get his hand back out of his pocket caused him to fall against the small end-table. Leroy threw another punch and clipped Eddie on the left side of his head. Eddie shook himself and attempted to shoulder-block Leroy to get himself away from the wall. Leroy turned Eddie's body to the right and swung him across the living room table and onto the side of the couch. Phyllis, screaming for the men to stop, heard her baby in the room crying.

"LEROY STOP! EDDIE STOP! Y'ALL ARE SCARING MY BABY! PLEASE STOP!"

Leroy turned his head toward her while pulling up his undershirt that was tucked in his pants, and shouted to Phyllis,

 "SHUT UP AND SIT DOWN!"

Eddie, looking at Leroy who was two feet away from him and Phyllis who was no more than two feet behind Leroy, kicked the table that was blocking him from getting to Leroy. He arched his back to throw a punch at Leroy but Leroy turned back and facing him pulled out a revolver with no energy to stop, pulled the trigger. Phyllis saw Eddie's head jerk back as a thin wisp of smoke between the barrel of the gun and the bullet wound to Eddie's chest, floated up to the ceiling. Eddie's body fell straight back knocking over the chair and onto the throw rug that was used to center the coffee-table.

There was silence for a second as Leroy dropped his arm to his side and wiped his lip with his free wrist. Leroy cracked a smile and stood over Eddie. He was now profusely bleeding from the wound in the center of his chest. Leroy turned to see what Phyllis was doing. He grinned when he saw how the look of fear and shock was plastered over her twelve-year-old face. He turned back to Eddie, who was barely breathing and had blood coming out of his mouth. Leroy knelt down over Eddie's body and placed the gun barrel to Eddie's temple.

Seeing this, Phyllis screamed,

"LEROY! LEROY! DON'T DO IT! DON'T KILL HIM!"

Before she knew it, Phyllis jumped on Leroy's back and tried to wrestle the gun away from him. Leroy stood up with Phyllis still hanging on to his back, but holding the gun away from her reach, walked away from Eddie's body and flipped Phyllis over his shoulder against the side wall. Phyllis tried to get up, but Leroy kicked her in the chest. He lifted up the gun and pointed it directly at Phyllis.

"I ain't gonna tell you this twice. Shut up and stay quiet or I'm gonna kill you and your baby. You hear me?"

"But, Leroy," Phyllis said crying uncontrollably, "we need to call 9-1-1! We need to call an ambulance!"

"We don't need to call anyone. You ain't calling 9-1-1 until after he's dead."

Leroy turned back to Eddie and kicked his head. There was no reaction. He knelt down and put his ear near Eddie's mouth, then slowly moved away. He put the gun to Eddie's temple, and looked at Phyllis.

"Leroy! Leroy... please don't kill him! Please don't kill him. Please let me call an ambulance! Please Leroy... please, don't kill him."

Leroy stared at Phyllis as he held the gun firmly to Eddie's head. He stayed there for a few more seconds then he moved the gun away. With his free hand he went into Eddie's pocket and removed all of the money, pulling out his wallet and scraps of paper from the other back pocket.

He patted down the pockets to make sure nothing was left. Then he pulled Eddie's body over and reached into his front pocket, taking out a set of car keys and a couple of other bills. He stared at Eddie for a second and smiled. Leroy stood up and waved his gun at Phyllis who was still sobbing in the corner. He pointed the gun in the direction of the room where her crying baby could be heard. Then he turned around and gently parted the curtains, peeking out of the living room window and quickly ran out of the house.

Trapped Between Two Mountains

From where she sat, Phyllis could see that the door wasn't fully closed, but she dared not move because she didn't know if Leroy was waiting there for her. She held her breath but in her mind, asking God to save her and her baby. Phyllis was about three feet away from Eddie, but only seeing the top of his head she believed Eddie was dead. She heard the rumbling of a car engine, a second later, the screeching of tires. Still, Phyllis was too scared to move. She wanted to throw up and she also wanted to reach her baby, but the sight of that gun stole her courage.

Minutes felt like hours. Her baby was still crying and she suddenly recognized the smell of her baby's bottle burning on the stove. She looked over at the top of Eddie's head, over his shoulders and the top of his feet. She stared at those areas hoping to see some movement. Then she heard the sound of children just outside the window. They didn't seem scared and the sound went past her house as if they didn't see Leroy or they didn't care. Phyllis slowly crawled to the window, but not past Eddie. She slowly knelt up. With every inch, she fought the fear of seeing Leroy's face pressed on the other side of it. She thought to herself, 'well, I could quickly bob my head up to see if the coast is clear. Maybe, if he is there, he will have his head turned?' She leaned up quickly and saw no car in front of the house. She took a deep breath and knelt up again looking from side to side. The coast was clear.

Phyllis felt her legs, but now she felt the urge to cry. She crawled over to the phone that was partially hidden by the couch and slowly called her Aunt Gladys.

For a moment, she couldn't remember Aunt Gladys' number. Her head was hurting and she was still breathing irregularly. The rotary dial came to a stop with the last number. One ring... three rings... six rings, as Phyllis was about to re-dial, the receiver lifted up.

"Hello?"

"Aunt Gladys?"

"Yes, ma'am? Who would be calling me at a time like this? Don't you know there's a proper time to be calling folk?"

"Aunt Gladys, it's me!"

"Me? Me, who?"

"It's me, Phyllis. Aunt Gladys... I... we... Leroy... come quick!"

"Child, what you talkin' about? You ain't making no sense. Is everything alright?"

"Nooooo, please come Aunt Gladys, please come!"

Fifteen minutes had passed since Phyllis hung up the phone. Her baby was still crying and the fumes of burnt formula became visible to her in the living-room. She heard footsteps coming up the walkway but feared it was her brothers and sisters. She was preparing to scream for them to get help when she heard Aunt Gladys call out her name. Two seconds later Aunt Gladys was looking across the living room from the doorway.

"OH, MY GOD! OH, MY GOD! LORD JESUS! OH, MY GOD!"

Trapped Between Two Mountains

Gladys had immediately held Phyllis and told her to stay right where she was. Gladys was careful not to look at the body when she went into the kitchen then into the bedroom where the baby was. She rushed back out and sat beside Phyllis.

*** *** ***

Gwen put the letter down after reading about Leroy's apprehension on the highway going to Eddiesville. She wondered how could things go so wrong with her mother and Leroy. She wondered if things would have been different had she been there.

Gwen finished her second cigarette then walked over to the sink and washed her face. She looked at herself in the mirror and made a promise. "I will never come back here as long as I live."

There was a knock on the warden's door. Blankenship was balancing the phone in her ear while pulling one of the bottom drawers open. "Millie, tonight's the night... yes, I have been so excited about it, too... I had my black blazer cleaned and altered just for tonight's show..." She pulled out a bundle of papers and began to sign a few and separate them into two piles.

Occasionally, she'd touch the tip of her tongue with a finger and turn a few pages with it. She'd repeat this pattern for the next few minutes as she continued her conversation.

"Millie... oh, I forgot to tell you. I just bought some black lace up's, they look like a short version of the ones that used to be popular in the twenties! They're absolutely exquisite. I think we'll be a matching pair! It's a pity you have to accompany your drab husband. Wouldn't it be delightful if it was just the two of us?"

There was another knock on the door.

"Come in!" Blankenship looked up from behind the piles in front of her to see the door as it slowly opened.

In walked two security guards, Officer Ward and Officer Crawford. Blankenship looked at her watch, looked at them and then looked at the phone. Officer Ward moved to the side and looked behind her to the hallway. She silently motioned with her hand and Gwen walked into the room.

Gwen's face was red and she had several scratch marks on her cheeks. Her hair was a mess and her blouse was ripped underneath the collar. When the guards walked her to the front of Blankenship's desk where she took a seat, Blankenship noticed that she wasn't wearing any shoes.

Blankenship put the receiver back to her face.

  "Millie... Millicent... I'll call you back in about an hour...oh, okay, I'll see you tonight then...yes, yes, I'm looking forward to it. You take care. Bye, now."

Blankenship put the receiver back on the base and straightened her lapel before leaning back in her chair. She slowly rocked back and forth. Blankenship stared at Gwen. She didn't take her eyes off of her. Gwen tried hard not to look back at Blankenship but she felt Blankenship's piercing stare, even when Gwen's focus was the view just above Blankenship's chair to the manicured lawn.

There was a sullenness that permeated the air for about five minutes. Only the sound of the second hand ticking and the portable air conditioner interrupted everyone's attention.

"Do you wonder why we're here again, Miss Collins? Doesn't it surprise you that we'll have to extend your stay here the more you get yourself into trouble?"

"But, Warden Bla-"

"No but's Inmate Collins. Just looking at you I can tell why you're here. Didn't I make it abundantly clear to you that you were to stay out of trouble? Oh, but I partially blame myself because I always assumed you were a sane person. So, tell me Collins, do you like it here? No, let me put it another way. Have you been institutionalized? I think you need to be institutionalized."

"No, I'm not psychotic. You think I want to get in trouble and be written up so that they can deny parole?"

"It sure seems that way."

Blankenship stopped rocking in her chair and pulled herself closer to the desk. She clasped her hands in front of her and sat them on top of her desk.

"So tell me...what is it now? Did someone talk crazy to you? Did someone talk bad about your boyfriend? Did someone steal your bag of pills? And, Oh... yes, I do know about the pills you and the others have been getting from the infirmary. I

know all about it. You see, I get a list of all the items that come into the compounds. Every... thing! And, I keep an inventory of every single item. Everything! I can tell you right now who's using pads and who's not and how much toilet paper each woman uses to clean herself."

Blankenship leaned back in her chair and clasped her hands behind her head.

"Collins, I can tell you who's sneaking into who's room. What they're doing and when they're finished. I know everything about everybody here. I have eyes everywhere, Collins. And, I mean everywhere. If I wanted to Collins, I can stand in each inmate's room and watch them and they won't even know I'm there. So, what do you have to say for yourself?"

Gwen was stunned by such an admission. She believed in a code of silence. She had to because it took her so long to earn enough trust just so that she could have a dialog with the inmates and even longer before they'd trust her to sit at the table to represent the Second Floor. She wasn't going to lose that by being a snitch, but with Blankenship staring in her eyes with a slight smirk, Gwen had to give her some information or she could find herself in solitary and/or even lose parole.

"I'm waiting Collins, what do you have to say for yourself?"

Gwen bent her head down and tried to remember how exactly did all of this begin?

*** *** ***

Trapped Between Two Mountains

The day started off like any other day such as the breakfast-call and chore duty. In this case, Gwen was assigned to washing dishes. (Gwen learned that the warden didn't want her doing strenuous outdoor activities like picking fruits in the hot sun in her condition.) There was also a few laps around the compound before returning to the cool of the house, but there was another reason that Gwen liked her daily walks: it cleared her head.

Gwen needed a clear head because she was about to play the third week of Spades and her team was up by 800 points. This type of spades, what the other inmates told Gwen, was known as Prison Spades for it's extended play and higher bid values. Nevertheless, Gwen wanted to keep the momentum going because if her team could win by a large margin, she would have felt vindicated in her self-boasting. It was a great start, she just needed to keep it going and judging by the score, her team would win the championship in about two weeks.

Gwen finished lunch and was looking forward to starting her hand. As she was gathering her lunch tray and utensils, she casually looked around the room and noticed that the two guards were not at their respective stations but by the window in the corner talking and pointing to something that was outside. When Gwen saw this, she turned to see what the other inmates were doing. A glance around the room revealed something very interesting. Although the guards were in the same room, the brief distraction invited inmates to openly (yet inconspicuously to the uninitiated) make deals for extracurricular activities. Gwen saw these deals by the passing of objects from one hand to another. A utensil dropped on the floor near another inmate who'd, in turn, take that item and place it in her waistband. There was the 'leaning over a conversation' and a 'hug of the shoulder' while something was being passed around in a concealed manner by hands outside of the guards' clear visibility. Gwen had seen it all. She smiled to herself because Jink had already taught her the tricks of the trade. What she was witnessing was quietly coordinated but nothing she hadn't seen up close in Charleston.

Gwen walked a few steps and put her tray on the dirty-dish row. She took one more look at the guards who were deep in a conversation to remember why they were there and decided to leave. She took just one step and found herself stepping on Terri's foot who had just walked in to get lunch.

 "*Watch where you're going,*" Terri said as her lips creased as it snickered.
"I'm sorry, I didn't see you."

Gwen looked at Terri with sympathy and tried to diffuse any new aggressive response.

 "*Don't think I don't know what you're doing, Collins. You ain't running things around here.*" Terri said as she poked Gwen in the forehead with two of her fingers.
"Look, I said I was sorry, but don't put your hands on me," Gwen said this as she started to backup.

Trapped Between Two Mountains

Wilhemena stepped in front of Terri and pointed in Gwen's face,

"I don't care who you think you are. This ain't Charleston and you ain't got no Jink to protect you. You just better watch your words."

Gwen took a step back,

"You think I'm scared of you? I'll fight you anytime and I don't care if I don't get paroled."

Terri brushed Wilhemena aside and put two fingers of her own on Gwen's face.

"I'd like to see you do that, pip-squeak!"

Gwen looked at her face, but in that moment she remembered when she first met Terri. She was sitting in a thunderstorm across the street from the Rite Aid on the library steps. She remembered opening her home to her and later introducing her to friends at Miss D's house, including Terri's future girlfriend.

All of those thoughts flooded Gwen's mind and she felt the pressure of Terri's fingers on her forehead. Gwen took a short inhale and with one quick turn of her shoulders, she reached up and grabbed Terri's intruding fingers and lowered them to her mouth and chomped on them.

Trapped Between Two Mountains

The more Terri tried to pull away, the more Gwen bit down even harder. Terri's head jerked back as the pain vibrated from her finger to her shoulder and to her chest. It wasn't long before the pain went into opposite directions. The only sound Terri was able to make was a mournful scream.

She lunged to Gwen's left side and started to punch her. She tried with her free hand to push Gwen head off of her now swollen. When nothing seemed to work to free her fingers from Gwen's bite, Terri started to pull Gwen's hair, pleading with Gwen to let go. That bundle of two women pushing and screaming and biting and kicking and pulling hair came to an end when the hands of the guards rested on their shoulders.

As they separated the women, one guard pulled Gwen aside, the other spoke to Terri. Gwen stared at Terri as her guard walked over to the table to pick up her notepad. Gwen motioned to Terri to keep the incident private. She mouthed the words, *"I'm up for parole."* Just as she finished, her guard stood in front of her again.

"Collins, I need you to look at me and not them. Now, I need to hear what happened from you."

Gwen looked at the guard then looked at the other group from the corner of her eyes.

"Nothing, it was just a misunderstanding."
"A misunderstanding? Is that right?"
"Yes, go ask Terri. She'll tell you the same thing."

"So, a misunderstanding has you looking like something that came out of a horror film and another inmate over there has a busted lip and clutching her hand."

"I ain't no snitch."

"Well, I hope for your sake they say the same thing. You know Collins, you have a good reputation around here unlike some of the other inmates from Charleston. It'll be a shame if we have to bring you to the warden's office."

The other guard came over and whispered something into her ear. Both looked at Gwen for a second until the guard assigned to Gwen tapped the tip of her pencil on her tongue and prepared to write.

"Now Collins, I'm going to ask you one more time. What's your side of the story?"

Gwen looked at them then looked at Terri. She stared at them and looked back at the guards.

"Nothing."

*** *** ***

"Okay Inmate Collins, I've heard your story... again. You're sounding like a broken record claiming that you're the victim here. But, I'll give you the benefit of the doubt since it was two of them and just you... and, I know that Terri has a temper. So, this is what I'm going to do and I'm letting you know that if I weren't in a hurry to go someplace, I would drop the hammer on all of you. Since you didn't own up to the situation and they did, I'm going to leave this as an infraction on your record."

"But, Warden-"

"No, don't but Warden Blankenship, me! My officers asked you repeatedly to tell your side of the story and you refused. That was the time to be cooperative, not when you find yourself sitting across from me."

Blankenship pushed herself into her desk and leaned into Gwen.

"Let me tell you another thing, Collins. These officers are my eyes and ears in this facility. They represent me. Everywhere you see these officers, you see me. Everything these officers say, I'm saying. I'm everywhere. I'm in the dining room. I'm in the field. I'm the voice announcing the mail. I'm even sitting in the stall next to you in the bathroom. I'm leaving this on your record and you can be assured that you'll most definitely fail probation the next..."

Blankenship leaned up and opened the bottom left-hand drawer and thumbed through a couple of manilla folders until she pulled one up. The protruding tab on the folder read: Collins, Gwen. She pulled a single sheet and there were a list of dates and some red marks check in the fail column.

"Ahh... here it is. I see that you have a parole interview coming up... next... what's today's date... you're up for a parole review next Thursday."

She turned the page around so Gwen could see it.

"See what it says, Collins?"

"Yes, ma'am. I know."

"You know? Collins, I'm going to be straight with you. I really do think you need to be institutionalized because anyone up for parole and still allows herself to get caught up in a scandal that she knows will cause her to lose this privilege has got to have something wrong with them."

"No, ma'am. I'm not crazy. I just don't want anyone to push me around."

"I see. So, you're your own enforcer as if these guards get paid to look pretty."

Gwen bowed her head and slowly bit her bottom lip.

"Collins, I'm going to tell you one last time. When my officers speak to you, you respond. If they ask you any question, you tell them what they need to know. That's it. You put yourself in this position because you didn't want to do what was lawful out in the public. Collins...I'm going to make this so clear that even a baby can understand it. I don't want to see you back in my office, your name on a disciplinary report or any other report that is bad in nature. You are one infraction from going into Solitary. And, believe me, when I tell you, not even Satan wants to be in Solitary. Now, take this as your last warning and let this be a lesson to you. Let them say whatever they want about you. Walk away. My guards call your name, you get your rump to them as fast as humanly possible. Crawford!"

"Yes, Warden!"

"Take Inmate Collins back to her room and let her get herself cleaned up. We're going to let her meditate on this warning but I'm also allowing her to go out and play her cards with her friends, to let her know that we are pulling for her and want her to leave our fair Pence Springs as a model, reformed inmate.

"Do you have any other questions for me, Collins?"

"No, warden."

Officer Crawford helped Gwen to get up from the chair and started to walk out of the office. The other officer walked a few steps behind but decided to close the door after them instead of going out. Blankenship noticed the returning officer approaching her desk, looked up.

"Yes, Officer Ward. How may I help you?"

"Warden, if I may ask. Shouldn't we have written up Terri as well?"

"In time, Officer Ward, in time. I suspect those two and others will get themselves into much bigger trouble than just fighting with Collins. Collins is harmless. She thinks she's tough and is willing to make a scene so that others don't mess with her. They'll snitch on Collins but they won't snitch on themselves. I let Collins go to let her think that she got off fairly easy, but what I really want Collins to think is that when it comes right down to it, she has no real friends. Or the friends she thinks she can rely on can't be trusted. Collins is going to tell us anything we want to know."

"You think the threat of solitary confinement will do the trick."

Blankenship leaned back in her chair, rocking for a second and smirked.

"There's no teacher like terror, Ward. There's no teacher like terror."

17.

Gwen stayed in her room after she took a shower and received some bandages and ointment from the infirmary. The guards, she noticed, took particular interest in her body language. She suspected they believed she was preparing for retaliation but Gwen shook her head in disgust. A few hours nap and she'd feel better, she thought, although Gwen knew she just blew her next parole hearing.

As she climbed into bed, she wondered why did Terri and Wilhemena snitch. Inmates don't snitch on each other, no more than we drop-dimes to the police in Charleston. What's wrong then, Gwen thought as she looked up at the ceiling.

She took a deep breath and touched her stomach. Gwen hadn't thought about Jink or about the correspondence that she wasn't receiving from him either during the affair earlier in the day. Gwen got up and went to the sink. She splashed water on her face a few times then dried her face with the towel. Then she left her room feeling shut in by her thoughts. She walked to the recreation room and saw cliques of women scattered about the room. In one area, the women resumed their Bid Whist competition.

She saw Terri and a couple of other inmates she knew by face but not by name talking and staring at her. She also saw Lola and Vivian sitting down at a table, as well as a guard standing up keeping watch.

When the guards noticed Gwen, she looked at her, then she looked at Terri and back at Gwen. It was clear to Gwen that all of the guards were informed about the incident earlier in the day and the repercussions in Blankenship's office.

Gwen shook it off only to see her friend Linda waving for her to come over.

  "Gwen, Gwen what happened? I heard people talking and they said you were in a fight over something. Some people said you started it, some other people said they attacked you. What happened?

*** *** ***

Linda Taggert was one of the few people who took to Gwen after she came to Pence. Linda was friends with Donna and would, on occasion, sit with her when the other inmates in her third-floor area weren't around.

After Donna left, Linda would occasionally come by and sit with Gwen and catch up on what has happened on her floor. Gwen always felt safe around Linda and always felt encouraged about her stay after she left. She promised herself she wouldn't lose contact with Linda the way she lost contact with Donna.

Gwen didn't remember what Linda said she was doing time for, but when she thought about it Gwen suspected it had something to do with embezzlement. All Gwen knew was Linda had all of the creature comforts of home in her room. She had a television, a radio, plenty of books and snacks.

For her part, Linda saw Gwen as a sister from the other side of town and whom she would ask the delicate questions about race and culture that she couldn't with anyone she knew personally. Linda often talked to her family, especially her mother, about Gwen when they came for visits. Gwen was surprised when Linda's mother came to visit her. Mrs. Taggert was the first and only guest to have visited Gwen the entire time she was as there. The visits were followed by commissary money and unexpected packages from the Taggert family.

As Gwen sat across from Linda, she wondered why this type of friendship couldn't be the rule in the country and not the exception.

Trapped Between Two Mountains

*** *** ***

Gwen looked at Linda.
"And, that's what happened. I can't afford to get into any trouble with them or anyone or Blankenship's gonna put me in Solitary."
 "She can't do that without any reason."

Linda had a look of distress of on her face.

"Blankenship can do anything she wants, she's–"

There was a hard knock at the entrance door. Officer Crawford used the handle of her black flashlight against the edge of the door. She took a step in the room and looked around.

"I need everyone to come downstairs to the dining room, right now!"

There was no movement amongst the women in the recreation room.

 "INMATES! Are you listening to me? I said, I need all of you to stop what you're doing and report to the dining room immediately!"

In every area of that large room, grumbling was heard. Officer Crawford crossed her arms and groups of women slowly walked past her. She ignored the obvious question spoken to her as the cue continued out the door.

Gwen and Linda were near the end of the line. Crawford overheard the conversation between Gwen and Linda as they passed by her.

"Linda, what do you think is happening?"

Within a few minutes, the entire second and third-floor inmates were gathered in the dining room. Although there were whispers about the cause, no one knew for sure what was happening.

As all of the inmates waited for some kind of announcement, Crawford came from behind two other guards who were blocking the entrance.

"What is she doing here?" Gwen whispered to Linda.

"I don't know, but by the looks of it, it can't be good. I've never seen her here this late."

There was silence as Crawford walked closer to the line of inmates who stood against the wall.

"COLLINS!"

Gwen froze for a second. She needed a second to cope with the fact that her name was just called. Why me, she thought, I didn't do anything wrong. Blankenship already punished me this morning.

"COLLINS! I SAID NOW!"

Gwen left Linda and approached Crawford from the farthest part of the room. She stood in front of Crawford in stone silence. Crawford stared her down from head to toe.

"Turn around."

Gwen titled her head in confusion,

"Turn around? What for?"

"Collins, you were given an order. This continued questioning of my authority will be put on your record and given to Warden Blankenship. Now, turn around."

Gwen turned around, then after a minute, turned around again to face Crawford.

"Collins, go to the bathroom, we'll be there in a second."
"To the bathroom!"

"Didn't I just warn you about disobeying an order? I see you didn't take heed to the warden's threat."

Gwen gave Crawford a hard look then slowly walked to the restroom. She looked around the restroom looking for some clue as to why she was there. She paced around thinking to herself, what did I do? She probed her mind but nothing seemed to make any sense. She heard the door behind her close. Crawford walked in and was fixing some medical gloves on her hands.

"Collins, I need you to stand right here in this spot next to the mirror and under this light."

Trapped Between Two Mountains

Gwen as about to question the order but looked at the expression on Crawford's face. She walked to the spot that Crawford pointed out and crossed her arms in defiance.

"Strip!"

"Say what! Strip?"

"I said, STRIP!"

"I'm not stripping!"

"YES, you are!"

"What for? I wanna know why."

"I don't need to tell you why. Just do as you're told, inmate."

"I'm not doing it until you tell me why."

"I don't need to explain anything to you. I'm going to give you one last warning."

Crawford moved her hand over to the baton that was sitting in one of the belt's holsters.

"I said, STRIP!"

Gwen, seeing the gesture, unbuttoned her blouse while sliding out of her shoes. Crawford, with her arms crossed, watched as a mound of garments piled up at Gwen's feet. Crawford motioned for Gwen to push the pile to a spot she pointed to then return to her standing spot.

"Why am I naked?"

Crawford said nothing as she went into her pocket and produced a tongue-suppressor from a thin package.

"Open your mouth and say, ahhhh!"

Gwen paused for a second then opened her mouth. Crawford had a small penlight that she used to look into Gwen's mouth. When she was finished, she threw the thin stick in the wastebasket.

"Raise your arms to shoulder-length and spread your legs."

Before Crawford finished the last syllable, she was already giving Gwen a hard look. Gwen raised her hands and spread her legs.

"But, why are you doing this to me? What did I do? I was just sitting down talking with my friend. I wasn't talking to anybody else.... awww, do you have to do that?"

Crawford stood back up, facing Gwen.

"Turn around and bend over."

"Bend over, no! I'm-"

"Collins, I said turn around and bend over."

Gwen felt her heart racing. She knew the threat of Solitary was real and was only a signature away from happening. Thirty days, she thought, thirty days locked in a room with no windows, no light, no one to talk to and only one bath a week. Gwen turned around, put her hands on her knees and bent over.

Trapped Between Two Mountains

As she looked at her toenails she remembered the last time she was in this position. She also remembered that 'feeling of invasion' stayed with her for several days. Now, to have a hostile officer's digits invading her was no less humiliating. When she felt Crawford's hand retreat, she stood up straight and turned around facing Crawford. She gazed over Crawford's shoulder but was really trying hard not to cry.

"Collins, you can get dressed now. Report to the living room and wait for further instructions. Do I make myself clear?"

Gwen said nothing as she reached for her panty.

Gwen walked out of the bathroom to find Officer Ward and a couple of other guards going through the same routine as it was with Crawford and herself. This concerned Gwen because it meant that something really, really big was happening and some inmate was about to be punished.

As Gwen was walking to the living room, she heard Linda's name called. She turned around to see where her friend was. Linda walked in the direction of Gwen on her way to the guard and said to Gwen:

"It's gonna be alright...I'll be just fine...we'll talk about it later. Please don't worry about me."

"I wanna know why we're here!"

Gwen shouted from the main couch in the living room. Two guards were standing in front of her,

"Buffy... Terri... Mary... Peeka Boo, you're next! Collins, we don't have to answer any of your questions. Your job is to follow orders. That's it."

"But, you have to tell us what's all this about. We deserve an explanation."

"No, you don't!"

"Yes, we do!"

Gwen looked at the two guards and saw the look of frustration on their faces.

"Collins, this is a routine search. We need to do this whenever it is deemed necessary."

"Well, I don't believe that. You didn't have to do all that, making us strip because you looking for something." Gwen said while staring directly into Officer Crawford's face. "I wanna talk with Miss Blankenship."

"You can, but Warden Blankenship's not here. You can address your concerns with her tomorrow."

"Tomorrow! I want to talk with her now!"

"Inmate, lower your voice. You don't make demands around here. You're in prison, don't you forget that. Now, to satisfy your curiosity, the warden is at some kind of opera... or classical performance tonight. She'll be back tomorrow."

Gwen took a deep breath. In the background she heard a couple of the other inmates grumble loudly, we want answers, we want Blankenship! Gwen looked over Crawford's shoulder while all of this was happening and noticed the expression of the other two officers. The expression of frustration turned to rage. One of the officers nudged Crawford in an act of wanting to take it from here but Crawford didn't budge, nor did she take her eyes off of Gwen.

"Inmate Collins, you had better stand down or face some serious consequences. I've had just about all that I can take from you. Now, go upstairs to your room and don't come out until you're given permission." Looking squarely at the other women beside Gwen, Crawford also said, "That goes for the rest of you. GO UPSTAIRS NOW!"

Gwen looked at Buffy to see what her expression was and all of the women quietly resigned to upstairs. As they filed out of the room, one of the officers looked at Gwen,

"We're gonna keep an extra eye out on you Collins. Don't think we're not going to report this to Blankenship."

Gwen was silent as she walked out the door but it was in the hallway where Buffy heard Gwen grumble,

"You can tell Blankenship what you want."

Gwen and the other women walked up the stairs, each at some point looking behind them to see where the guard was before they attempted to say anything that may be in earshot of her. Gwen was still grumbling even louder with each step she took until she reached the top step of the second floor. However, the image in front of her took her breath away.

Buffy, walking up the stairs right behind her, tapped her to keep going. When Gwen turned to look at her, Buffy was shocked to see Gwen's silent expression. Buffy squeezed herself into the small space on the other side of the step where Gwen stood and Buffy put her hands to her mouth.

"Oh... my... god...." Buffy said.

Both women saw what was the equivalent of a hurricane hitting the second floor.

"Gwen, what happened?"

Before Gwen could reply, doors to the inmates' rooms began to open and the faint shrills of screams echoed from the cracks of the doors. Personal belongings from each room were scattered all over the hallway. Some inmates' room doors were slightly ajar, while others were fully open. Every single item of clothing, containers, mattresses, toiletries and even portable radios were thrown to the ground.

Both women walked slowly as screams hysterically were heard behind the doors. They saw some inmates kneeling on the floor crying. Some were looking at torn garments, others were picking up radios with broken parts, a couple of women sat on the floor holding their heads in their hands.

Gwen stepped into one doorway when she didn't see anyone from her view and saw Vivian holding Lola. Lola's room was trashed beyond recognition. Her room, by Pence's standards, was the gold seal of luxury for all the inmates. It looked better than any master bedroom Gwen had ever seen in any magazine, but it was totally demolished. Gwen overheard Vivian tell Lola that everything was going to be all right and that she was there to take care of her. Gwen stepped back from the doorway and walked briskly to her door down the hall.

Trapped Between Two Mountains

She arrived at a partially opened door where she saw a few of her bras on the floor. She carefully pushed the door open. Everything she owned and those provided by Pence was on the floor along with her bag of clothes, her portable radio and the box with all the letters she received from Madisonville including the unfinished letter she received from her Grand-Aunt Gladys.

Next to the overturned box and underneath the left foot of her favorite three-inch heels was a broken picture frame. The glass front was shattered and the small string, which was used to hold the frame to the wall, was severed. To the left, a photograph of her mother Lila Mae and her grandmother, Cecil and herself as a little girl was bent with a shoe imprint on it.

Gwen reached over the picture and brushed off the speckles of glass that were on it. She tried to flatten out the picture by rubbing it across her chest, but the crease was still evident. She held the picture in front of her and began to cry.

Gwen stood up with the picture in her hand and looked around to the disaster of her room. She took a few steps on the bare spaces of the floor to get to where her bed was, but the sight of her room was too much to bear. She held the picture with her lips and lifted the mattress back onto the box spring, straightening it in the process. She rested the picture on the edge of the bed and was about to sit down when the rage of this moment overcame her.

She walked across the room to the doorway all the while trying to suppress the questions that were flooding her mind. She wanted answers. She needed answers to explain why her whole life was now dismantled and thrown at her feet. She had to be appeased and nothing short of that was going to do.

Gwen marched out of her room and walked past the women picking up their clothes in the hallway and in their rooms, where voices were now calling her name. She turned around when she recognized one of the voices being Buffy's.

"Gwen! Wait! Where are you going?"
"They gotta tell me what's going on. They can't do this to us! This ain't right. Look at us! They destroyed our rooms... they went through everything I got!"
"Gwen, I know! Don't go and do anything stupid!"
"They can't get away with this. This ain't fair. I'm not gonna let them get away with this. Y'all can stay here, but I want some answers."

Just as Gwen turned to go downstairs she heard several women behind her agreeing with what was just said. Gwen heard some women telling her to wait because they were coming with her. When Gwen reached the bottom of the stairs, she was followed by about eight other women including Buffy, who wanted to protect Gwen from what was going to happen. They walked to the living-room and sat on the same couch where they just sat fifteen minutes before. The guards were off to the side of the room and didn't initially notice them until they overheard some chatter behind them.

Officer Crawford walked over first followed by two other officers. They stood in front of the couch in front of Gwen and the other inmates with the arms crossed. Crawford put her arms out and held the other officers back as if to say she was going to lead this conversation.

"Inmates, what are you doing down here? Didn't I tell you to go to your rooms?"

Gwen looked at her.

"You had no right to trash our rooms. Didn't we do what you asked? Why did you have to go through our rooms and throw everything around?"

"Inmate Collins... I already explained to you that this is a routine procedure to ensure the safety of all of the people who are here at Pence. It is not your right to question or to challenge any decision made by the staff here. If we want to go through your rooms, we can do so at any time and you won't have anything to say about it."

"I won't? Officer, you must have me confused with someone else. You're not going through my things like it don't matter. I want to know ('we all want to know,' was heard beside her) why you did that? What you looking for?"

"Collins, I told you before I don't need to answer your questions. You got all the answers you're going to get and more because I'm writing this infraction up and reporting it to the warden tomorrow."

"Good! Write whatever you want. I want to talk to Blankenship! I want to get to the bottom of this!"

"You seem to have forgotten our little conversation with the warden just this morning. I think you do need to be

institutionalized. I didn't before but now I see the warden was right. You do act crazy."

"You can call me whatever you want but I ain't leaving until I talk to Warden Blankenship!"

"Oh, you're not! Inmate, I'm giving you and I'm giving each of you an order. GO BACK TO YOUR ROOMS RIGHT NOW!"

"I'm not leaving until I talk to Blankenship, myself. So go and do what you gotta do, but I ain't leaving."

Several of the other women beside Gwen said the exact same thing verbatim. Only Buffy didn't mouthed the words back to the officers. She stared straight ahead as to tacitly agree with the other inmates in silence.

"INMATES, I SAID, GO TO YOUR ROOMS. NOW!"

Gwen turned and repositioned herself on the couch as to face the other inmates and at the same time, turned her back to the officers. She started small talk with the other inmates and would occasionally tell them not to worry about the officers behind her.

Crawford looked at her watch and told the other two officers,

"We have some more staff coming. They should be here any minute. I'm going to the office to make a few phone calls, stay here and keep an eye on them and let me know the moment Officer Bowling arrives."

The other two officers nodded in silence, then Crawford walked off.

Crawford walked slowly out of the living-room, but quickly picked up her steps when she was out of sight. She wrestled a gaggle of keys off of a belt loop and opened the door to the main office in front of Pence's entrance.

She looked through scraps of paper looking for the warden's emergency contact number. There were several numbers, most of which were numbers for her home and for close relatives. She pondered for a second about approaching the family when she knew that Blankenship was looking forward to this performance for months.

She also knew that Blankenship had her handheld radio with her but would probably have the sound turned to silent in the theater. Her heart raced as to what to do. She worried that if she called Blankenship and she deemed it not an emergency that would affect her review rating.

Crawford also thought about the possibility that Blankenship would think this happened on her watch because the inmates considered her weak and ineffective. Crawford concluded that she had to assert herself first then call Blankenship with a follow-up. She couldn't be seen as weak in anyone's eyes, especially Blankenship if she wanted a promotion.

Crawford hesitated to call for formal back up because she heard over the shortwave that a state trooper was ambushed and was currently in ICU while the police force was on a manhunt. She needed reinforcement but it had to sound urgent or they'd delay sending over officers. She picked up the telephone and dialed the direct number for the sergeant.

"Hello... yes, sorry to disturb you. This is Officer Crawford at Pence Springs, I'm in command of the outfit while warden is away on personal issues. We have a situation where a group of inmates has staged a sit-in. Yes... Blankenship, yes... Crawford. There are about eight inmates. We had to do a room search for items stolen from one of the new nurses and perhaps items from the infirmary. Yes... we've apprehended the inmate but some of the other inmates became enraged with the handling of the matter and have decided that they were going to take over one of the wings of the institution. Yes... they're huddled in the main room and they're making a list of demands including an audience with the warden... yes, we've identified the leader as Collins... Gwen F. Collins. Yes, that's right... on drug-related charges and probation violation... yes, she does look capable of violence. Thank you. Yes, I will.

Crawford put down the receiver and was about to walk out of the office to talk to Officer Bowling who'd just arrived, when she remembered she needed to talk with the warden. She picked up the phone and dialed emergency services and sent a message to about the situation and the state troopers.

She knew it would be a short period of time before the warden would call, she just hoped that the police would arrive before then.

Trapped Between Two Mountains

When Crawford left the office, she saw one of the officers in the hallway in front of the entrance of the living room talking with Officer Bowling. Crawford overheard Bowling calmly pleading with the officer not to call the state police because she could defuse the situation by talking Gwen and the other women into returning to their rooms.

"Too late Officer Bowling. I had to make a judgment call and we gave the inmates plenty of time to think about their decision and more than enough time to return to their rooms and put their belongings together."

Officer Bowling looked at Crawford,

"Why did it have to get to this point? If you knew that Collins and the other inmates were innocent, why involve them in the first place?

"Officer Bowling, at the time, we hadn't apprehended the suspect and we couldn't take the chance that those individuals were not stealing pharmaceutical and resold to each other.

Inmate Collins took it upon herself to be the leader of this rebellion. We had no intention of letting it go any further but she became resentful and challenged my authority. I suspect under the circumstances that the warden would have let the infraction go because she was innocent and the warden does favor her. But we can't allow insurrection. That puts your life in danger as well as our own."

"So, you called the district police?"
"Affirmative."

"And... the warden?"

"Affirmative."

Officers Bowling, Crawford and another walked into the living room where another officer was standing beside the Gwen and the other inmates. As the officers looked at all the prisoners Crawford looked at her watch and walked to the window, which displayed the front of the building. She parted the drapes and seeing nothing, she looked again at her watch. Just as she was about to close the drapes she saw three prisoner trucks pull up in the driveway. She closed the curtains and walked past the other guards out of the living-room to the front door.

Gwen peeled her eyes and saw someone from outside peeking into the room.

"Hey, wait here. Someone's outside, I gotta see who this is!"

Gwen walked to the window where Officer Crawford was just looking out. When she got there, she saw a troop of heavily armed policemen running into the building. Gwen came running back to the couch.

"Hey, guys, guess who's outside.... the police! Ooh, somebody's in trouble!"

Gwen sat on the couch and started laughing with the other inmates when both of the doors to the living-room was fully opened. Crawford was standing in front of nine police officers with riot gear on. Some had batons in their hands, others had their hands on cans of mace and one had his hand on his gun.

Trapped Between Two Mountains

Crawford looked at the policeman in front of the group and pointed to Gwen.

"THERE SHE IS, RIGHT THERE!"

19.

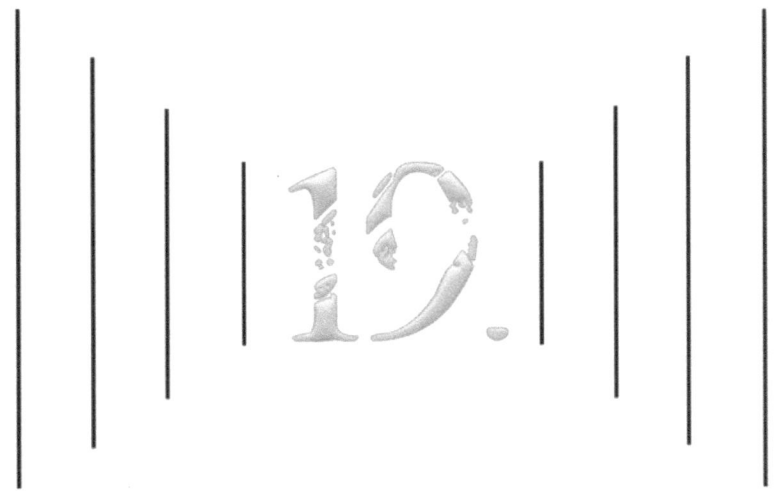

"THERE SHE IS, RIGHT THERE!" Officer Crawford said to the head of the riot squad.

"She who? What!" Gwen said, in a stunned posture.

The police captain took out a baton and took a step in Gwen's direction as the other policemen in riot gear pulled down their face masks and approached the women next to Gwen.

"YOU!" The police captain screamed at Gwen.

"Me! What!" Gwen said, as she instinctively walked backwards toward the other inmates.

"GWEN, WHAT DID YOU DO? WHAT DID YOU DO?" One of the inmates said as they jumped up from the couch and started to back up to the rear wall with the large fireplace.

Trapped Between Two Mountains

"I DON'T KNOW!" Gwen screamed back.

Gwen looked quickly around to see all of what was happening. She saw Crawford backing up in the opposite direction. That's when she thought to herself, 'This can't be good!" The menacing looking police, the usually bold Pence guards retreating to the safety of the background told her that whatever was about to go down, it was going down and in this room.

"GWEN... GWEN.. GO TO YOUR ROOM!" A familiar voice yelled to her, but she didn't know where it was coming from.
"NO, NO... I'M NOT GOING UNTIL I SPEAK WITH BLANKENSHIP!" Gwen shouted in the direction of the voice.
"GWEN, GO TO YOUR ROOM BEFORE SOMEONE GETS HURT! PLEASE... GO TO YOUR ROOM!"

Gwen looked around to see who was talking to her while keeping an eye on eight burly men in full riot gear with their weapons drawn, approaching her and her female-resistance crew. In the corner of her eye, she saw Officer Bowling talking to her with outstretched hands.

"Gwen... PLEASE... go to your room!"
"Miss Bowling, I can't. They can't get away with this."

Gwen felt the end of the room arrive when she couldn't take another step back. The troopers had now cornered the other inmates and with their sheer size and equipment, the inmates looked like school children being corralled by professional football players.

Gwen put her hands behind her and recognized she was standing in front of the fireplace. She looked forward again and saw one of the policemen rapidly approaching her. She felt the wall and discovered the poker leaning nearby the metal partition. Before the policeman could reach within striking distance, Gwen started swinging the poker back and forth.

"STAY BACK! STAY BACK!" Gwen shouted to the officer.
 "STOP GWEN! STOP! PUT IT DOWN!" Bowling screamed.
"NO! I DIDN'T DO ANYTHING!"
 "GWEN, I KNOW. PUT IT DOWN. YOU HAVE TO LISTEN TO ME!"
"NO! STAY BACK." Gwen swung more wildly.

The police officer, who was just a few feet away, felt the breeze of the sharp tip of the poker as it moved barely an inch away from his face.

 "GWEN! PUT IT DOWN."
"NO, MISS BOWLING! THEY CAN'T JUST COME UP IN HERE LIKE THIS!"

Gwen's attention shifted back to the policeman in front of her. She didn't see Miss Bowling approaching her from the side.

Trapped Between Two Mountains

Gwen mustered up her strength to swing at the officer as hard as she could but she didn't have a counter-measure to stop the poker from hitting Miss Bowling and sending her to the ground.

It seemed like a scene from a horror film playing out in slow motion. Aerosol cans that could only be mace and a handgun on the other side of his belt holster left nothing to the imagination. She had seen this type of situation play out before, only it was from the sidelines and she was rooting for the Men-In-Blue to take charge of the situation. How did she find herself on the opposite side of this story? The Man-In-Blue, wielding a baton in her direction, was no hero. Everything in her view seemed topsy-turvy. Miss Bowling was at her left, screaming and pleading with her. Behind Miss Bowling was Terri struggling and antagonizing another police officer while holding on his baton. In the center of the room, Buffy had her one hand on her waist and a finger in a policeman's face. On Gwen's right, but in the front of the room, an inmate was laid out on the floor with her legs up in the air across an overturned couch. Where the other inmates were, Gwen didn't know.

Gwen heard a lot of stories about police brutality or using way more force than necessary to subdue an individual. Even as a little girl, there was a neighbor who had an altercation with the police and his face was bandaged pretty heavily for weeks. Even after the bandage was off, his face never looked the same and he now spoke with a lisp. Everyone knew this man to be a gentle, non- aggressive type, who's indiscretion happened to be that he was a happy drunk.

Gwen determined in her mind that if this was the modus operandi of the police, she wasn't going to go down without a fight. If they hit me, I'm gonna hit them back. I'm not going to be someone's punching bag, Gwen said to herself as the policeman attempted to grab her.

After the first few swings, she realized the poker intimidated the officer, but she knew she would tire herself of swinging. And she knew the policeman also knew this. Gwen just needed space to communicate to someone who'd call them off, but in the heat of the moment, clarity of mind was absent.

As Miss Bowling pleaded with Gwen, Gwen saw the policeman ready to leap for the poker handle. She knew that he was after her and her only source of protection. She turned from Miss Bowling, and in the direction of her strongest arm, she swung for the policeman's head. The sharp-pointed poker looked like the head of a medieval spear. The point missed the tip of his nose by mere inches. He could see and feel the wind of the blade across his face.

The momentum of the swing also swung Gwen's four-foot, five inch frame all the way around. It was like the poker had a life of its own and Gwen was just going along for the ride. In a split second, Miss Bowling had walked two feet closer to Gwen, but it was two feet too close.

Gwen felt the impact of the poker against Miss Bowling's shoulder. The impact also woke Gwen out of the fuzzy awareness of rage to the present moment of fear and grief.

Gwen dropped the poker and ran over to the fallen guard, who was clutching her arm and crying hysterically.

The police officer pulled Gwen off of Miss Bowling and slammed her against the floor. He reached behind Gwen and held her arms behind her back as he pressed his knee against the back of Gwen's head.

The body-slam against the floor rattled Gwen as she felt the left side of her face ache with pain. Gwen struggled with the pressure of a headache and the weight of this man on top of her. Gwen had no movement, save her eyes. It seemed as if Miss Bowling's injury turned up the policemen's anger and aggression.

One officer grabbed Buffy by the hair and dragged her a few feet before he used her hair to catapult her body against the wall. Terri was no less fortunate. When Gwen last saw Terri, she was struggling with a policeman's baton. Gwen laid on the floor bruised and bleeding from her mouth and nose, she saw Terri screaming profanities at the officer. The officer turned around as if he was leaving, only to turn back and hit Terri with a right cross to the jaw. A dazed Terri still held on to the baton, but greatly shaken.

A few more words were exchanged and Terri was on the receiving end of another hard right cross to the jaw. Terri let go of the baton but tried to punch the officer. The officer dropped the baton back in his belt and waited for Terri to swing. The officer's last punch was an uppercut in the exact same spot as the first two blows. Where Terri fell, Gwen couldn't tell.

Gwen's neck was now throbbing, she had trouble breathing,

"Get off of me. I can't breathe…. I can't breathe, you're killing me."

"SHUT UP, INMATE. I DON'T WANT TO HEAR ANYTHING FROM YOU." The officer kneeling on her back said.

Some of the other police officers allowed a couple of Pence's guards to help Miss Bowling to the Infirmary. As Miss Bowling was being helped out, Gwen saw Bowling saying something to one of the policemen, then pointed at her. The guards then put their arms around Miss Bowling and they went through the door.

One of the guards walked up to Gwen and he knelt down beside her. Gwen could only see his shoes.
 "I don't want you saying anything. Just nod to my question."

 Gwen didn't say a thing.

 "Are you pregnant, Inmate Collins?"
 "No. My baby's with my momma."

The policeman stood up. He still held her arms in back of her but he helped her to stand up.

 "You're pretty much in a pickle, Inmate Collins. We're leaving you here at the discretion of your warden. She'll have something to say about it in the morning. In the meantime, we're taking you upstairs, where you'll stay in your room until a decision is made about what happened tonight."

Gwen stared straight ahead.

"I suggest that you behave yourself for the rest of the night."

The policeman nodded to the remainder of the officers who were still there in the living-room. Every officer held an inmate's arms behind her back and dragged them up the stairs, except for Terri, who was carried by the arms by two policemen. She hadn't come to yet.

Gwen was taken to her room and pushed to the floor. The policeman and a Pence officer locked Gwen's door as they did with the other inmates. Gwen looked around at the room and knew that if she looked at her face, she wouldn't be able to tell which was worse.

She crawled on the floor, grabbed the nearest shirt and pressed it against the swollen side of her face. Then she took it away to look at the imprint of the damage. Spots of perspiration and blotches of blood soiled the beautiful white shirt. She blew her nose at the bottom of the shirt and saw more blood in the mucus. She crumpled the shirt and threw it away from her.

She reached the bed and saw the picture of her mother and grandmother. She stared at it for a second, but this time, a speck of blood fell on the picture. Gwen tried wiping it away with her finger but she only managed to smear it. She felt frustrated with herself because she just ruined the picture.

Her eyes were burning from blood seeping into them and she was unable to stand without falling back down. She noticed the commode a few feet away. It took her a minute but Gwen took a deep breath and leveraged her weight against a few pieces of clothes that were nearby and hoisted herself above the rim of the commode.

She peeked over and was relieved that the water was clear. With each palm-full of water, the remnant became increasingly crimson in color. After four splashes of water and ignoring the irritation of the open wounds on her face, Gwen exhaled and sat upright on the toilet with a soiled tee-shirt rolled up in her hand.

For the first time in hours, it felt great just to feel her chest expand and deflate and to listen to her heartbeat. Just then, she heard a rattling of keys at her door. The jingling of keys echoing in the hallway caused Gwen to look. She stopped her thoughts from speaking to her as she turned to the door.

She heard the scrape of the iron key pushing through the lock. The handle moved up and the door opened swiftly. Officer Crawford and the captain of the riot police stood in the doorway. The sight of them gripped her and immobilized her.

Only the movements of her thoughts were free, and they spoke fear. What's happening? Why are they back? What do they want? All of these questions raced through her mind and the questions constantly repeated themselves in her mind. She thought she was free of the police, but in walked the Pence guard, and the police officer. They saw Gwen sitting on the floor beside the toilet.

"Inmate Collins. Get up! You're coming with us."
"What! What is this about?"
"Inmate Collins, this is no time to question me, just get up and come with us."
"Where are you taking me?"

The guard nodded to the policeman and he walked over and grabbed Gwen pulling her up. Gwen started screaming and threatening to call the governor, Charleston magistrate Carol Fouty, legal services, the newspapers. She struggled with the policeman and then Crawford came over and tried to grab one of her arms.

Gwen lashed out wildly at Crawford and the policeman. As she turned her head away from Crawford, she only had enough time to see the clenched fist of the officer speeding toward her face. Gwen felt his knuckles penetrate her left cornea and she fell unconscious to the ground.

She was awakened a few moments later as she felt herself being lifted up by the officers. She heard Crawford tell the riot policeman that she would have preferred to leave Gwen here and let her recover from her wounds, but she had to follow orders given to security by Blankenship.

"Where are you taking me?" A groggy Gwen said as a throbbing pain gripped the side of her face. The officers didn't respond.

With only partial vision in one eye, the last thing Gwen saw as she was being carried out of the room was the picture of her mother and grandmother on the floor. She saw drops of blood all over it.

COLLINS... COLLINS... GET UP!" Officer Crawford said as she shook Gwen's shoulders. *"COLLINS... I SAID, GET UP! NOW!"*

Gwen lifted her head up as much as she could before a wall of pain in her neck stopped her from going any further. It was easier for Gwen to lay on the cold, hard floor than for her to get up. Gwen heard some rustling just above her, then she felt two hands slide underneath her shoulders, grip her armpits and yank her up.

Gwen looked over to one side and saw a patch of blood drizzling down his hand and long, gooey mucous drain on his forearm. Then she turned to the other side to see Crawford's hand under her other armpit. Her vision was blurry from the swelling, but when she looked up at Crawford's face, she could see the vast, blank, emptiness in Crawford's eyes. It was almost as if her soul was a big, empty room that no one had visited in quite a while.

"Collins, stand to your feet. We're not carrying you!" Crawford said with a steely stare.
"Where are we going?" Gwen said between inhales.
"I said, stand to your feet, inmate! I don't have time to pander to your childish whims."
"I'M NOT GOING!" Gwen screamed while pulling and pushing both the policeman and Crawford.

As Gwen screamed, yelled and cursed, the policeman looked at Crawford in her eyes and spoke directions without vocalizing the words. Gwen was then lifted and dragged out of the room. Threats of calls to the governor, calls to the newspapers and local television stations echoed down the hall as Gwen twisted and jerked in every conceivable way she could think of.

They reached the end of the foyer then carried Gwen up another flight of stairs. Gwen was surprised that not one was curious enough to see her protestations from their doors. She was hoping to have at least one witness whom she might call upon to verify police brutality. But no door opened.

They reached the landing and Gwen was still kicking and screaming. Her plea, "Where're y'all taking me", still went unanswered. They dragged her to the end of the hall where the policeman wrapped both of Gwen's hand behind her back.

Gwen couldn't make out what was in front of her. The nondescript door hand no markings on it, but it had a large, double door handle just above the standard Pence prison door lock.

Crawford stood in front of the door. Gwen was about five feet directly behind her with the policeman firmly holding her arms. Gwen heard the thump of the lock bolts then Crawford returned the keys to her waist. She turned to the police officer and nodded.

"WHAT IS THIS? I AIN'T GOING! LET ME GO! I'M GONNA REPORT THIS TO THE NEWSPAPERS! I'M GONNA CALL MAGISTRATE CAROL FOUTY!"

Crawford turned back to the door, pushing down on both handles as she opened it.

"I'M NOT GOING! LET ME GO!"

The door opened to a large room; perhaps the largest room by length, and inside, all other inmates of Pence Springs sat quietly. Crawford took a few steps in then turned to the officer and nodded. Gwen struggled and kicked.

"I'M NOT GOING! JUST WAIT, I'M GONNA CALL-"

The officer lifted Gwen up. As she was brought to the doorway, the expression on her face changed. She looked all around the room and saw all of the other inmates from both floors. Gwen looked behind her to the policeman.

"What are you going to do with us?"

"INMATE, I'M TIRED OF YOUR MOUTH. SHUT YOUR MOUTH!"

"NO, YOU SHUT UP! I'M NOT SHUTTING UP UNTIL YOU TELL ME WHAT WE'RE HERE FOR!"

Crawford turned to Gwen,

"COLLINS, GET IN HERE RIGHT NOW."

"NO, I TOLD YOU I'M NOT GOING. I'M GONNA CALL-"

The policeman looked at Crawford and mouthed the words, *"Help me get her in."* Gwen was able to get her hands free and held on to the outside wall, preventing the door from being closed. She kicked one of her legs free and hooked it on the opposite side of the doorway.

"HOLD HER BY THE WAIST, LET ME GET MY HAND FREE!" The officer yelled at Crawford as his wrist was grabbed by Gwen.

Crawford endured slaps and pushes and a few colorful names before she was able to grab Gwen by the waist. Crawford held Gwen but turned her head toward the inmates in the room, who were now standing a few feet away from the doorway watching intently.

"INMATES, GET BACK TO YOUR SEATS OR THEY'LL BE AN ADDITIONAL 60 DAYS IN SOLITARY FOR ALL OF YOU!"

The inmates stepped back as they saw the policeman pull out a silver can with some obscure marking on it. The policeman maneuvered his arm from around Gwen's upper torso and neck to her face. Gwen was screaming and reaching for the policeman's face. The officer pushed up Gwen's eyelid with a free finger and sprayed the contents of the can into Gwen's exposed eyes. The piercing scream made many of the inmates' scream and cry themselves, as Gwen continued to threaten to call the newspaper offices.

The entire room was now filled with the terrorized voices of the inmates. Some screamed at the police officer, some screamed at Crawford while others screamed at Gwen. For it was Gwen, whom they thought, would cause this issue to escalate to even more violence.

"GWEN, SHUT UP! GWEN SHUT UP!"

Before the other inmates knew anything, the sound of heavy boots came rumbling into the room. They looked up and saw a contingency of riot police with masks on, holding the same kind of can that was used on Gwen.

"GO!" Screamed the police captain. And in one swift motion, the battalion of officers covered the air with mace. A few seconds later, the entire room was cloudy.

One by one all of the inmates stumbled, crawled or had to be helped from that large waiting room floor. The gas was so thick you could slap it, flip it or kick it, if you wanted to.

Trapped Between Two Mountains

They stood. They sat. They kneeled. They coughed. They Vomited. They Cried. They rubbed their eyes and tried to wipe away the long, elastic film that was draining from their noses. One by one, the officers in gas masks grabbed an inmate underarm and escorted them outside the room. The air in the hallway outside was only marginally cleaner than the room everyone just fled from, but no one noticed that Gwen was still inside.

Moment's later, two officers with masks on walked inside and carried Gwen out by her arms. As they came out to the doorway leading to the hallway, the first officer motioned to another who was outside to make room for them to come out.

The police in the hallway began to push the inmates back a few feet. They also told the inmates through their masks, to remain as quiet as they possibly could.

Gwen was slouched over between the two officers with her head down. The first officer turned and pulled Gwen up.

The other inmates could still hear Gwen grumble and swear but they surmised that she wasn't ever going to be completely silenced, so the guards would have to live with that concession.

Gwen lifted up her head when she felt a burst of fresh air greeting her in the hallway. Her vision was almost completely blocked. She didn't see the faces or the expressions of shock and terror that was about to visit the other inmates when they saw Gwen's face. She knew something was very wrong though when she heard some of the other inmates scream and cry.

"Is it that bad?" Gwen faintly said to the crowd in front of her.

The police sat Gwen down upright against the wall. She felt their steps walk away from her, but she knew they were still close. She heard parts of their conversation about the rooms Blankenship had on-reserve for emergencies needing to be double-checked. Gwen put her hands on her face and as she moved her hands up to where her eyes were, she carefully followed the bulge. With the tip of her fingers, she realized what the other inmates were screaming about: her swollen, infected eyes had protruded further out from her face than her nose. Her eye sockets were so inflated, the space between both eyes was lost.

She was about to ask for medical attention when a familiar voice spoke in front of her.

"Well, look what you did! You couldn't keep your big, fat mouth shut! Now, we're all headed for solitary for the next sixty days thanks to you! And all we got to show for it is a whoopin' by the police. You can't see me, can you?" Terri inquired.

"No. I can't. I can't feel my eyes. It feels like somebody rubbed my eyes on a dirty carpet. But, I know it's you, Terri."

"You do, huh?" Terri said with cold, blank stare. "How does it look?"

"You look like Cyclops. Your whole face is swollen but your eyes are so swollen that you can't put on shades because you don't have a nose right now."

"How's everybody doing?"

"How do you think we're doing? None of them want to talk to you. I'm the only fool and that's only because you were there for me when I needed someone. So, now that favor has been repaid"

"I never did anything for a favor. I just wanted to help you get on your feet."

"Well, regardless. I'm putting a target on my back if you start your stuff again. I won't be able to help you."

"Is anyone hurt like me?"

"Well, let me see...."

Terri turned around and saw three troopers and two Pence guards turning the corner. She looked at the other inmates then turned to Gwen.

"Well, it seems like you got competition. I can't speak for everyone but just looking around, I can see some of the battle scars on people like Dorothy H, her arm's broken, for sure. Pia... her nose looks like it's broken... and... and... what's your friend's name... the white girl with the long black hair?"

"Buffy!"

"Ahhmmmm. Well, that white girl got the worse of it."

"What happened to Buffy?"

"They're taking her someplace, but they ripped out her hair in the back. She completely bald in the back. She looks like one of those old women in the retirement home who forgot to straighten their wig when they'd go out for a walk. It wouldn't

surprise me if they took her in the back room and slapped some Windex on that bald spot!"

"BUFFY! BUFFY!" Gwen called out.

Gwen heard some new steps come toward her and Terri.

"INMATE. You've caused enough trouble. I suggest you be quiet before we take even more extreme measures."

"I just want to know how my friend is."

"I think you need to be concerned with the trouble that you're already in. As a matter of fact, you and this inmate that you're talking to have to come with us."

"Where?"

"Don't worry about where. Just stand to your feet."

Gwen and Terri walked down the hall, where they saw the tall, red steel door. Both women hesitated at the sight of it but the troopers tugged on their arms, pushing them forward. The red, steel door! It was as intimidating to see in person as the stories told by other inmates made it out to be.

Gwen whispered to Terri,

"It's gonna be alright. You'll make it."

"That's easy for you to say. I'm not used to getting into trouble," Terri responded.

Over the course of a few days, with bare bone sandwiches for breakfast, lunch and dinner, each of the inmates were called and removed from their rooms and taken to the hospital for treatment. When Gwen inquired about when would it be her turn, she was told that she'd be called when it was her turn.

After almost a week, Gwen found herself in a room with Buffy when Terri didn't come back to the room. Both women cried at each other's injuries and predicament and promised each other that whatever it would cost, they would always have each other's back. Early one morning both women heard the key to their door. Buffy described who was at the door to Gwen while she helped Gwen to sit up. Officer Crawford told them that it was their turn to get medical attention and they'd be leaving immediately for Summers County Hospital.

Buffy following Crawford held on to Gwen and led her through the maze of the building until they reached the ground floor. They reached the car and sat in the backseat. Gwen had mentioned to Buffy on the way down the stairs that she hoped she wouldn't need surgery for her eyes. Buffy replied that she hoped the doctors wouldn't tell her that her hair loss was permanent. Both women felt optimism and a bit of anxiety at the same time because they had given up hope that anyone from the medical community would see them and treat them.

Buffy gripped Gwen's arm as the car pulled out of Pence's driveway.

"Don't worry Gwen, everything's going to be all right. We're going to get through this. We're strong women."
"I'm glad one of us feels that way."

Trapped Between Two Mountains

Buffy said little, focusing her thoughts on her breathing and not letting Gwen know that she too was a bit scared of what might happen. And, she wanted to know if she was at liberty to talk to the hospital staff about the confrontation several days ago. She'd occasionally look at Gwen but wouldn't stare at Gwen's eyes. It looked far worse that what Buffy had been telling her about the improvements.

The car drove through areas that Buffy was unfamiliar with. Buffy started pressing her face against the window looking for something familiar, but nothing was. She felt Gwen touch her arm.

"Buffy is everything all right?"

Buffy didn't answer Gwen but leaned up and spoke to Crawford who was sitting on the passenger side of the front seat.

"Officer Crawford, where are we going?"
"I told you where we're going, didn't I?"
"But, this is not the way to Summers County. We should have been there already. Where are you taking us?"
"Buffy, what's going on?" Gwen said as she too leaned up.

Crawford stared at Buffy for a second then turned around and looked straight ahead. The car continued on its path for another forty-five minutes. Buffy was now holding Gwen tightly. Gwen felt her friend shaking and sobbing. She knew that Buffy had reached the breaking point. Now, it was her turn to show strength.

"Officer Crawford... Officer Crawford"

"Yes. What is Collins?"

"Officer Crawford, I can't do anything to you or to anyone else. I can't see... and I don't pose a threat to anyone, but can you please, be honest with us about where we're going. It's clear to us that we're not going to the hospital. Please tell us where we're going."

Crawford turned around and saw Buffy shaking and her eyes red from crying.

"Officer Crawford, please! I know you don't owe me any favors and I know I messed up! If we're not going back to Pence, can you at least tell Miss Bowling how sorry I am? It was an accident. I just want her to know that she treated me fairly and I'm so very sorry about everything."

Crawford looked at Gwen at that moment.

"I'll make sure to tell her. For what it's worth, she pleaded for you and Buffy to stay to the warden. She was never, not looking out for you. She forgave you for hitting her immediately."

Crawford turned around and continued to stare out the front window.

"Officer Crawford," Buffy spoke, "could you please tell me what we did wrong for you to take us away from this place?"

Crawford saw the sorrow in Buffy's eyes then looked at the damage to her scalp,

"Inmates, I'm not supposed to tell you exactly where we're going. That was my instruction. I was told directly to take you to another location. I'm sorry. I really am. I'm very sorry."

Gwen put her hand on the seat in front of her.

"Miss Crawford, please tell us."

"Collins, I'm sorry. I'm really, really sorry."

"Why are you apologizing?"

"I'm sorry. I'm sorry. That's all that I'm at liberty to say."

Buffy and Gwen sat back against their seats. The car slowed down approximately twenty minutes later in a rural area in Staunton County. The car drove through a path onto a large multi-building complex with pillars at the front of each building.

As they approached what could be mistaken for a college campus, Buffy saw a sign just up ahead.

"Oh, my god... Oh, my god, Gwen! They're not taking us here?"

"Here, where? Buffy, where are we?" Buffy looked at Gwen,

"The sign says, Welcome To Western State Hospital. They're taking us to an insane asylum!"

"*Turn around Collins, let me take off the handcuffs.*" Crawford leaned down and uncuffed Gwen. "*Stand behind Braxton and wait until you're called. This is NOT Pence and they won't tolerate your rebelliousness here.*"

Gwen stood behind Buffy as she tried to see through the small opening in her eyelids. Buffy was her eyes in the ride over but now she would have to find a way to see again on her own. Over Buffy's shoulder, Gwen could vaguely make out Officers Crawford and Ward talking to several Western State officers. They stood in a semi-circle before Gwen and Buffy, each party exchanging glances with each other after looking in Gwen and Buffy's direction.

Crawford pointed to Buffy and handed a small stack of papers to one of the officers. Then that officer passed the packet of papers to a woman sitting behind a glass window that looked like a ticket booth at a movie theater. The woman stamped each of the papers then detached the first few sheets and returned the rest to the officer. The officer then signed the top sheet and handed it back to Crawford. They repeated the steps with Gwen's case file, except Gwen's file was about twice the size.

This time, Crawford handed the file to the officer with a nod, looking in Gwen's direction. She leaned into him and whispered something before stepping back to the place where she was standing. The officer looked at Buffy then directly at Gwen with a stern face before initialing the top page and handing the bundle to the woman behind the glass.

While the transfer was going on, Ms. Ward kept a careful eye out for Buffy and Gwen. But everyone knew if there was a hiccup in this order, it would come from Gwen. After the officer received the bundle back, she handed the packet back to Crawford, who then handed the papers to Officer Ward. Ms. Ward put the papers in a folder and wedged it between her arm and her side.

Both Ward and Crawford nodded their goodbyes to the institution's officers and walked past Gwen and Buffy without saying a word. Even Gwen's question, How long are we gonna be here, went unanswered. Gwen and Buffy stared at the women as they got into the car and watched as it started to pull off, too afraid to turn around and face their future.

"Which one of you is Braxton?"

One of the officers said while holding a small packet of papers in his hand.

"That's me!" Buffy said as both she and Gwen turned around to see the voice that just spoke to them.
"Come with me over here."

Buffy turned around to see Gwen.

"Don't worry about her. She'll be alright. We're going to ask you a few questions and then you'll visit our medic and then you'll go to your room."
"Why am I here? This place is for crazy people, I'm not crazy and neither is Gwen."
"I didn't say you were. I just need you to answer a few questions that one of our coworkers will ask."
"Why can't I go to the hospital?"
"We have a doctor on staff and she'll be here in a few minutes. This is only a routine procedure."

As Gwen was eavesdropping on that conversation, she saw the outline of another officer off to the side holding another packet of papers in her hand.

"Collins!"

"Yes, ma'am?"

"I'm Officer Jones, please come with me."

"Where are we going?"

"You'll know in a minute, but I must inform you that I know of your reputation as a troublemaker. I need your cooperation and everything will run smoothly. Your tendency to be disruptive, I assure you, will not be tolerated."

Gwen said nothing.

"I can see that your eyes are injured. We're going to take you to see someone who'll give you some medication for your eyes and some sedatives to relax you. But first, I'm going to take you just a few steps away from here and have one of our office deputies explain the rules and regulations here. You have to understand how things are done around here or you'll be lost. Do I make myself clear?"

"Yes, ma'am. But... may I ask you a question?"

"Yes, Collins. Just one, because we need to get you situated before lunch time."

"Why are we here and not at the hospital?"

"This is a direct order from your warden. We have specific instructions that we have to follow. You're not here by accident."

"Wait-"

"Collins, we need to go. Put your arm out and I'll lead you to talk with this officer."

Gwen put her arm out and the officer led her to a desk in a room around the corner. She sat down facing the instructor while the officer stood in the back of the chair. The voice in front of her spoke very softly and slowly reading the rules and regulations. After each paragraph Gwen was asked if she understood what was just read. Gwen would nod in response. When they were done, the deputy compiled all of Gwen's papers in one pile.

"Now Miss Collins, we won't call you Inmate Collins on this campus, but we need you to understand that the rules are meant for your protection and ours. Do you have any questions before we take you for a your medical exam and show you to your room?"
"Yes! I want to know why am I here? No one ever told me or Buffy what we're doing here."

The deputy took a deep breath and then looked in the file she just compiled. She flipped through a few pages then looked at Gwen.

"Miss Collins, it says here that you were convicted of murder and that you became restless and disruptive to the point of starting a riot at Pence."
"THAT'S A LIE! THAT'S A LIE... THERE WAS NO RIOT!"

The officer put her hand on Gwen's shoulder, gently holding Gwen from standing up.

"We were sitting down in the living-room, waiting to hear from Warden Blankenship and the next thing I knew the cops were surrounding us!"

"We have a different account of what happened. Warden.... Ve..Velma... Black-"

"Blankenship!" Gwen interrupted.

"Blankenship... yes, Blankenship. Velma Blankenship. Well, your warden has provided us with a document that says you were convicted of murder and that you're a threat to the other patients, to personnel and even to her. She notes that you were trying to intimidate so that she'd give into your demands. She says, here, that she recommends solitary confinement because she considers you a flight risk."

"THAT'S A LIE! OH, MY GOD, THAT'S A LIE... I HAVE...."

"Collins, calm down. Lower your voice." The officer behind her said.

"But, that's a lie."

"I'm only going by what she sent to us. Obviously, you did something that resulted in your condition. She also said you initiated some kind of riot and that you purposely banged your head against a wall when you were instructed to go to your room. As a result of your resistance, several other inmates became agitated and attacked the staff and the state police."

"Oh, my god! She's such a liar!"

"Well, if it's a lie, what happened to your face?"

"I never killed anyone. I don't like weapons and I've certainly never held a gun. Look at me! Do I look like a murderer?"

The deputy took a deep breath.

"Anyway. Collins, I also have to say that we have to put you in a segregated ward for special residents."
"Special meaning what? Hardened? Dangerous?"
"It's for your own good. Trust me, Collins, I don't want to do this anymore than you want to go. I don't have a choice. These papers say one thing and whether or not I feel if it's accurate is irrelevant."

Looking up to the officer behind Gwen,

"Okay, you can take her now. Make sure that she gets her three eye drops a day in addition to the approved medication."

Gwen quietly stood up when the officer tapped her on the shoulder. She was led out of the office and through two sets of security doors. When the officer opened the last door, Gwen was unprepared for the scene that was playing out in front of her.

*** *** ***

Western State Hospital, also known at other times as The Trans-Allegheny Lunatic Asylum, was one of the oldest and largest facilities built for the mentally insane in the world.

Trapped Between Two Mountains

The main building was the largest hand-cut stone masonry building in the United States and second in the world behind one built in the Kremlin in Russia.

Approved by the Virginia General Assembly in the early 1850's, the hospital was designed to house two hundred and fifty patients, but decades later and through the Civil War and The Great Depression periods, the hospital grew to house more than twenty- four hundred people in the 1950's.

In the late 1930's, a group of medical organizations funded a research project to learn about the efficacy of the treatments given at Western State. The study revealed that the hospital was a dumping ground for several state and local agencies for groups of people whom they deemed undesirable such as epileptics, alcoholics, drug addicts and the mentally retarded.

In 1949, The Charleston Gazette published a series of reports stating that WSH had substandard sanitation, insufficient furniture, lighting and heating in most of the complex. The facility was only modestly renovated by the early 1970's when Gwen and Buffy passed through its doors.

*** *** ***

The door opened to dozens of women walking around in nightdresses, soiled, dingy nightdresses. Some women dragged their feet while staring at the floor and grumbling to themselves. Others moved quickly in circles that made Gwen's blurry vision dizzying painful. Some women were laying on the floor looking up at the old, chipped painted ceiling telling the birds not to poop on them.

"Come on over here, Collins. We need to get some eye drops for you while you see the nurse."

Gwen was silent. She was trying to make sense of the image of people around her and the mixture of scents that would make even the most cast-iron stomach sick. She immediately thought to herself, how did the nurses and assistants deal with this smell all day. The combination of the two made Gwen self-conscious of her injuries even more. She thought to herself, she needs to develop a new game plan to protect herself. This was a different environment and a different kind of evil that lurked here.

From the door, the officer led Gwen to the nurses' station on the right side. Several of the patients bumped into Gwen on the way there. Each time they leaned into her to get a better look, the fumes of their unwashed underarms and the decaying food particles that stained their teeth made Gwen jerk her head in the opposite direction gasping for air.

The officer looked at the other residents and gently pushed them away from Gwen and told them to go. A few steps later, Gwen stood in front of the nurses' station. The hard, plastic seat was no more comfortable at the back of the building as it was in the front.

Gwen heard some grumbling in the back of her while the officer was walking with one of the nurses' assigned to Gwen.

But then, Gwen heard an even stranger noise coming from behind the woman. She couldn't make out what it was from the distance but one thing was clear, whoever it was and whatever it was that was being said, it was coming in Gwen's direction.

Suddenly the presence of the speaker was right behind Gwen; although Gwen couldn't see her, she knew it: she felt it.

"You redheaded whore, you stole my children! You redheaded whore, you stole my children! You redheaded whore, you stole my children!"

The voice continued that chant but turned from behind Gwen and started walking in a different direction. Her racing heart now felt a bit of comfort in knowing the danger had subsided.

"Collins, don't pay any attention to that. There are quite a few patients here with mental disorders. They're harmless if you ignore them. Let me introduce you to one of the nurses' on staff: Nurse Brady."

"Hi Gwen, I'm Nurse Brady. I'm one of the nurses on staff during the week. You'll come here three times a day to get these eye drops that I'm about to give you. And, once a day, we'll give you your prescriptions to help you settle down."

"Nurse, what kind of medicine are you giving me? Because I don't normally take medications."

"Oh, dear! It's nothing to be concerned about! Believe me, it's nothing harmful. It just makes you feel relaxed and sleep easier."

The officer, who stood at Gwen's side, stooped down and spoke directly into Gwen's ear.

"Collins, I need to get back to the office, I'll check up on you later to make sure you're comfortable. Now just remember what we talked about and everything will be fine."

Gwen said nothing but heard the officer's footsteps disappear in the background.

"Now, Gwen, I'm gonna take your blood pressure and your temperature. Just relax...great...you're doing just fine...."

"YOU REDHEADED WHORE, YOU STOLE MY CHILDREN!"

Gwen jumped up.

"Missy... Missy, Go! I said, Go! Leave her alone. Go! Be a good girl and go!"

The nurse cupped Gwen's face in her hands.

"Gwen... Gwen... you can sit back down now. You're going to be alright. We have a few... interesting people here. They're harmless, trust me. If they weren't, I wouldn't be here. Oh, dear! Your blood is high. Okay! Let's take your blood pressure a little later. I have some prescriptions for you."

Gwen heard her walk to a cabinet and heard the sound of cabinet drawers opening.

"Okay, I'm handing you a little cup. In it, you have four pills. You can take all at one time or you can take them one at a time. I have a cup of water for you as well."

Gwen took the little cup and popped the pills in her mouth. She extended her hand for the cup of water and quickly put it to her mouth.

"Great! Gwen, you're going to feel so much better in a little while. If there's anything I can help you with, don't be afraid to ask. Alright, I'm going to take you to your room and lucky for you, it's only a few feet away."

Gwen stood up and turned away from the nurse. With her back to the nurse, she reached up with her left hand and quickly grabbed the pills that were underneath her tongue.

"We ask the patients to leave their rooms in the morning because we lock the rooms during the day. We do this so we can keep an eye on everyone. Then at night, everyone can return to their rooms. We would then lock the rooms for your safety until morning. But, since this is your first day here, we're going to let you put your things and get acquainted. In about an hour, I'll come for you to show you around and give you a more formal introduction to this floor."

Nurse Brady came for Gwen exactly as she said. She carefully walked Gwen down the hallway. At each point, she made it clear where this room was in relation to Gwen's room or to the recreational area.

Trapped Between Two Mountains

The recreational area, an open area with a tv on the wall, several scattered chairs and a sofa was immediately around the corner from Gwen's room. After that, several more patient rooms and at the end of the long hallway stood a long table. This table was a makeshift dining room table. It was where the staff would leave the meals for the patients.

From the table and walking back, on the left was a sizable restroom that contained three stalls, a shower and a window that overlooked the campus' acreage. After this, there were three rooms patients deemed too dangerous to be allowed to roam for more than a few minutes. This was a 23.5- hour, confinement. Of the three available rooms, only one was in use.

Gwen inquired about the resident in the room and the nurse, after a few seconds of mental deliberation, simply said,

"Her name is Marcia."
"Marcia! Am I going to have to protect myself from her?"
"No, dear. Marcia is more of a threat to herself, more than anything else."
"How will I know what she looks like with my eyes like this?"
"Dear, don't worry. We normally let her out for a 10-minute smoke break. You'll see in a few minutes, all of the residents, even some of the more challenged, give Marcia her space. Do you smoke?"
"Yes, ma'am. Do you have any Kool Filtered Kings?"
"Well, I'm not familiar with that brand, but whatever one the officer brings up, make certain that when you get close to the

end of your cigarette that you put it out immediately and hide it until you're able to discard it away from Marcia."

"Can I ask you a favor, Nurse Brady?"

"Sure, dear! What is it?"

"I came here with my friend, Buffy. When do you think I can see her?"

"I don't know. That is a very good question. I'll try to find out for you. But, it would help if I could tell them that you've been a model resident. Do you think that's going to be possible?"

"No, ma'am. I'll be good."

It was a shorter break than expected when Gwen heard a knock on her door. Nurse Brady knocked again then stuck her head in the door.

"Gwen?"

"Yes."

"It's time. I need to bring you out so we can lock your room door."

Gwen walked out of the room and past Nurse Brady.

"We're going to have lunch soon but I think the assistants may have a cigarette break first for those who smoke. The cigarette break is usually about ten minutes, but the residents seem to be more relaxed afterward."

"That's nice. I could use a cigarette right about now."

"I would caution you, Gwen, especially with us trying to help you to heal from the fight you had, that smoking in excess.... I mean smoking, in general, is not really good for you. But we don't want too much cigarette smoke going into your eyes. We have to keep them clean as possible."

"Oh, okay. I'll try to be careful."

As they walked to the recreational area, the nurse tapped Gwen on the shoulder.

"Over there on your left is the guard station. If you cannot find us, you can go right there for assistance."

"Okay."

The nurse nudged Gwen to turn right to an open space. But it was in this open space that Gwen felt different personalities looming. Her impaired vision, notwithstanding, only complimented what she was now feeling inside of her soul. She felt the attention of people in the room with whom she could not see. She felt like a target. The impressions on her felt like arrows that were shot through the air. Whenever she felt a strong impulse coming from a particular direction, she'd turn to see and with the sliver of sight she had, she saw the images of the people looking in her direction.

Feeling these impressions, Gwen also noticed that she found it difficult to hear her own thoughts.

"AT THE CROSS, AT THE CROSS, WHERE I FIRST SAW THE LIGHT/ AT THE CROSS, AT THE CROSS, WHERE I FIRST SAW

THE LIGHT/ AT THE CROSS, AT THE CROSS, WHERE I FIRST SAW THE LIGHT...."

The sound of the chant coming directly behind Gwen made her jump. She heard this voice coming from the back of her on the right side and continuing until the voice was now in the back of her traveling left. The voice had reached a point where it wasn't getting lower from the distance, but the voice maintained its volume. Gwen surmised that this woman had reached the end of the room. Gwen suddenly felt a sense of empowerment, feeling that her hearing was a reputable substitute for her sight.

"Gwen, I'm going to sit you right here. Just put out your left and kneel just a bit. Right! There you go... we're going to get some cigarettes for everyone and then afterward, lunch will be served. I'll be back in a few minutes."
"Okay."

Gwen listened hoping to hear who was around her but there was a breeze that passed by her face. It was wispy figure, no more than four foot eight, four foot nine. The figure turned around and jumped into what had to be that mysterious chair in front of the smokers' circle. But, who is this person? Gwen stared in her direction but she looked like a ghostly figure watching and studying people as they went about their business.

"DOG, DOG, DOGGIE, PETER ASSHOLE! DOG, DOG, DOGGIE, PETER ASSHOLE! DOG, DOG, DOGGIE, PETER ASSHOLE..."

Oh, my god, Gwen thought to herself. This can't be happening. They're everywhere!

Before she knew it, the chorus would include two other women who knew about a dozen words between them.

"AT THE CROSS, AT THE CROSS, WHERE I FIRST SAW THE LIGHT/ AT THE CROSS, AT THE CROSS, WHERE I FIRST SAW THE LIGHT"

"YOU REDHEADED WHORE, YOU STOLE MY CHILDREN/ YOU REDHEADED WHORE, YOU STOLE MY CHILDREN/ YOU REDHEADED WHORE, YOU STOLE MY CHILDREN"

"DOG, DOG, DOGGIE, PETER ASSHOLE/ DOG, DOG, DOGGIE, PETER ASSHOLE/ DOG, DOG, DOGGIE, PETER ASSHOLE!"

They canvassed the cigarette area in unison and repeated their phrase undisturbed by the assistants who were putting cigarettes on a small tray. Gwen wanted to scream but the thought of a cigarette was too tempting to let go if she could just hold on for a few more minutes. Besides, she soon realized she was essentially trapped on a floor with two security doors.

"Okay women, please have a seat! Ladies, please have a seat if you want a cigarette."

Gwen heard a rush of footsteps from all directions grab chairs all around her. The voice that made that announcement was standing just above her and Gwen felt his hand on her chair.

"You must be Gwen!"

"Yes."

"My name is Officer Derek Hall, you can call me Officer Derek. I'm one of the assistants here, if you have any concerns or if there are any conflicts, don't hesitate to come to the office."

"Officer Derek, I can't see very well. My eyes are almost completely shut. I know I have to be out of my cell all day. Is there a chair near a wall that I can sit in without having to worry?

"There's quite a few. I'll take you to one where there's very little traffic."

"Thank you so much. Can I ask you a question?"

"Sure, what is it?"

"Is there any sane people here I can talk to?" Derek laughed,

"Yes, I know what you're referring to. We do have a young woman. She chose to keep to herself for the same reasons you're asking. I believe I saw her go to the restroom a few minutes ago. I'll introduce her to you. I think you'll be friends. She's here for different reasons like yourself."

"How will I know her?"

"Her name is Linda. I know you two will hit it off well."

Trapped Between Two Mountains

The bed was uncomfortable. With each turn, the rusted coils in the mattress echoed in the dark room, but after about few days, Gwen became acclimated to it. The first night, the shock of being at Western State, the cold, hard sound of the security doors slamming behind her, the stench of patients and the residual pain in her eyes and head was too much for Gwen and so she stayed awake all night. The days had gone by and the bed didn't feel as stiff and the pillows didn't seem so flat. This night, the fatigue of the long day made her body and emotions succumb to sleep.

Trapped Between Two Mountains

****

In the early morning hours, Gwen saw herself clapping and singing in church. She saw her grandmother, Cecil, in the choir waving to her. As she looked around, she saw Mrs. Jones hugging another man but she didn't recognize the man as being Mr. Jones. Mrs. Jones and the gentleman walked out of the pew headed toward the exit, Gwen saw Cecil suddenly standing at the door shaking everyone's hand as they left the service.

Cecil shook the gentleman's hand but hugged Mrs. Jones. She touched Mrs. Jones' belly and said a few words to her, then both of them laughed. She hugged Mrs. Jones once more just before Mrs. Jones walked out of the sanctuary.

Cecil saw the last person in line was her granddaughter. She leaned down and hugged Gwen tightly. They walked through the exit but instead of being in the lobby, they were on the road to Cecil's house. Gwen shook her head in confusion but couldn't find the question to ask her grandmother. Cecil stopped and looked at her.

"Gwen, I know what you want to ask me." Gwen looked at Cecil with a blank look.

"I want to ask you something but I forgot. It was something, but I just can't remember now."

"Does it have anything to do with Mrs. Jones and the man who was with her?" Cecil asked.

"I think so... maybe."

"Well, to answer your question. No, that man wasn't her husband but yes, that is their baby."

Gwen stood shocked. She looked at Cecil, but the words had froze her ability to think. She looked and wondered to herself, where was Mr. Jones and could something like this have happened. She just saw Mr. and Mrs. Jones together the other morning going to work and everything seemed fine, as it always is.

"Gwen, sweetheart, that's not a matter for you to be concerned with. That issue is between the three of them and The Lord. The good thing is that she decided not to stop the pregnancy."

"What do you mean stop the pregnancy? How do you stop being pregnant?"

Cecil gently grabbed Gwen's hand and continued walking to the house. They came to the front of the house but before they took a step in, Cecil looked at Gwen and touched Gwen's stomach.

"Gwen, when you start to have children, remember one thing: People inherit blessings that they aren't even aware of when they bring people into this world."

Gwen looked into her grandmother's eyes and saw the love of her grandmother streaming down her face.

****

Trapped Between Two Mountains

Gwen heard the lock turn on her cell and for the first time in several weeks, she was able to open her eyes without having to prop them up with her fingers. The fuzzy, blurry image of the room's door was remarkably clearer. The door opened and one of the assistants peeked in..

"Gwen, it's time to get up."

Gwen sat up and looked at the woman.

"I can see you."

"What!"

"I can see you. You have shoulder-length auburn hair. You have some freckles on your nose and you have some reading classes around your neck."

The woman quickly walked in.

"Let me see your eyes for a second. They're more opened than they were yesterday, that's for sure but-"

"OUCH!"

"Okay, they're still a bit swollen but that's okay. This is wonderful. I'll check with the attendant nurse but I think she'll still tell us that we should continue with the eye drops for the next couple of days. This is wonderful news, Gwen!"

"I wondered what you looked like," Gwen commented. "You're beautiful."

"Why, thank you, Gwen! My husband stopped complimenting me a long time ago."

"That's men for you!"

"Don't I know it."

The assistant helped Gwen to her feet. As they walked to the door, Gwen turned and picked up a towel and her toothbrush for her morning shower. But as she was walking to the door, she felt a soft hand touch her stomach. It felt like Cecil's hand in the dream she just had as if she felt an impulse on her fingertips. Gwen looked around the room before turning around and walking out of the door.

It was the first time that Gwen walked away from the nurses' station by herself after receiving eye drops and her medication. She held the towel and in the folds of her fingers were the pills she had just slyly spit in them when the nurses turned their heads. Gwen quickly turned and walked down the hallway to the restroom.

Gwen felt her heart racing because now it seemed as if she were over a hump and not stuck in a foxhole waiting for the artillery fire to stop. She was now over the embankment and was thinking to herself that she's in a position to work on getting out. A burst of excitement flared in her.

She turned into the bathroom and saw one of the patients kneeling down over the commode. It looked for a moment that she was vomiting, but the patient reached inside and quickly shoved something into her mouth. Gwen turned her face before she could see what the patient looked like and ran down the hall to call for the assistants. Gwen was hyperventilating at the thought of describing what she had just seen. All she could do was to point.

Two assistants wearing white sneakers ran to the restroom while Gwen leaned against the corridor wall. A few moments passed when the assistants turned the corner holding the patient underneath her arms. Their heads were turned in the opposite direction and they were both holding a wet rag underneath their noses.

Gwen walked slowly to the restroom and saw the efforts of the assistants to clean the area, but Gwen knew the janitors would actually do the cleaning. Gwen looked around to see if any of the other assistants were coming to the bathroom. When she saw no one in the hallway, she walked to the window that was just slightly off-center from the entrance. And on her tippy toes, she reached up to the windowpane near the lock and started feeling around.

She felt the pills she had left there since day one but made more space with her fingertips. She gathered the pills in her hand and placed them in her grip. Again, she tippy-toed to the spot where she just made space and placed the new set of pills there.

Gwen stepped down and as she turned to go to the shower, she saw a redheaded woman standing right behind her. The woman didn't say anything for a second but took a step in Gwen's direction and pointed to her:

"YOU REDHEADED WHORE, YOU STOLE MY CHILDREN/ YOU REDHEADED WHORE, YOU STOLE MY CHILDREN–"

Gwen sensing it was going to be a one-sided, long conversation brushed the woman and walked into the shower. The lukewarm water felt like a hug in that moment. As she washed her face, she realized that she could finally talk with Linda about the things she really wanted to talk about.

Gwen dried herself off and walked into the recreation area. She turned into the area where she always walked to by memory and saw Linda waving to her. Somehow, Linda knew Gwen was able to see what she fully looked like.

"Gwen! Gwen! Let me see your eyes!"

Linda had a big smile on her face.

"I walked past you at the nurses' station and I overheard you tell her that you could see. Yah! How does it feel? Can you see me more clearly?"

"Yes! You're prettier than I imagined." Gwen lowered her voice a bit, *"Girl, we have a lot to talk about!"*

"Boys, again?"

"No, but you know we got to yap about the opposite sex girl!"

"Okay, shoot!"

"Well, I had been thinking. You said you were sent here by your mom because she told the authorities that you were using drugs but it was really about a man, right?"

"Yep, that about sums it up."

"Well, that's exactly why I got locked up. They could have just let me go, but they had to teach me a lesson because I wanted to be with my man."

"That's my story to a tee."

"What if we wrote a letter to a judge or a newspaper explaining our situation and hope that someone looks into it.?"

Linda looked puzzled,

"Who'd we write to?"

"I don't know yet, but we gotta get outta here. You and I are not crazy and we don't belong here."

"I know that's right."

"Have they said anything to you about writing letters to someone outside?"

"No, I wrote to my father and he wrote me back just yesterday. He also sent me some commissary money."

"Okay, well they told me that I can't have any correspondence with anyone outside until further notice. I don't even know what happened to my friend, Buffy. One of the nurses promised that she'd look into seeing if we could meet. But, I haven't heard anything else about it."

"What would we write about?"

"We could tell them about the stuff that's going on in here."

"Okay, how do I tell them about my boyfriend or do I just say that the fuzz and my parents sent me here for smoking a joint?"

"The cops made a move on that excuse?"

"My parents didn't like my boyfriend cause he's colored and Hispanic."

"What?"

"Oh! I'm sorry. Am I supposed to say black, instead? I don't know."

"No, no! I'm not talking about that. I mean, your parents are that mean that they had to send you to an insane asylum for liking someone from a different race?"

"My mother told me that I had better not get pregnant or they'll disown me."

"For real?"

"Yep. Can I ask you a question? I'll get the letters mailed: one for you and one for me but you have to write them. I get confused when I write and my penmanship is bad."

"Okay. Deal."

"And, if either of us gets out first, we'll send commissary money to the other. Deal?"

"Deal."

Gwen and Linda shook hands.

"COLLINS... COLLINS!"

A voice behind the women called out across the room. Gwen turned around and saw one of the assistants calling her. Linda helped Gwen to her feet and Gwen limped over to the doorway where, as she got closer, saw Buffy standing by the assistant.

"Collins, you have a guest. We can't let you talk too long but because you've been a model patient, we wanted to reward you."

"Buffy!"

"Gwen!"

The assistant told them that he'd give them half an hour but that he'd have to take her back after that.

Neither of them heard the last statement as they both hugged and cried. Gwen was too excited to show Buffy that she could see out of both her eyes despite the fact that her eyes were still swollen and sore. Buffy, very gently, touched the swollen areas.

"Ouch! It's still very tender but I can lift my eyelids now. They hurt if I try to lift them too far back. I can see your hairs' growing back. It's looking real good. You'll have all of your hair back in no time. I'd say no more than two weeks."

"You think so?"

"I know so."

"I want to tell you something in private. Where can we go and sit down?"

Gwen looked at the assistant.

"Is it okay if my friend sat down with us and have some girl time before you take her back?"

Trapped Between Two Mountains

The assistant looked at Gwen, then looked at Buffy who had her hands pressed together in a prayer gesture.

"Yeah, sure. Why not! But I can't give you any more time. I have to get you back before lunch time and the cigarette break right after."
"Thank you, thank you, thank you!" Buffy said.

Gwen and Buffy walked quickly to that area that Gwen and Linda reserved for themselves. Gwen introduced Buffy to Linda and vice versa. Then Buffy looked over her shoulder to see where the assistant was.

"Gwen! Guess what! I was talking with one of the assistants and I found out that we can file a complaint with this agency because of the physical abuse. They may be able to set us free!"
"Free as is what?"
"I mean, we can get out of here and out of Pence... for good!"
"Oh, my god!"
"We've got to write to them and tell them about our situation, then they'll investigate and take our case."
"Well, how do we pay them?"
"It's free! These are people who help the poor and they get experience."
"Oh, really. Do you know how we can contact them?"
"I got it right here!"

Trapped Between Two Mountains

Buffy reached into her pocket and pulled out a slip of paper. The note read, Appalachian Research and Defense Fund, AppalReD in parentheses.

"Okay, let me work on it. I'll get a letter out for the both of us. If you can get a letter out, do it! I can't stay here any longer."

"I will, I promise. Don't give up, Gwen. We're too close to going home."

The assistant came back and tapped his watch. Gwen and Buffy stood up and gave each other a long hug.

"I'll come back to see you soon," Buffy said.

Gwen couldn't mouth the words to say, "Don't leave me." She just waved as the assistant escorted her out of the recreation room. Linda held Gwen's hand as they both sat back down. Gwen showed Linda the piece of paper.

"This is our ticket out of here. These people are gonna get us out," Gwen said but was still chocked up with sorrow.

"How?"

"I'm gonna write three letters, one for you, one for me and one for Buffy. I'll give you both letters tomorrow. You mail them under your name. Now, remember, since I'm writing to them, if you get out first, make sure to send me something from outside. I'll do the same for you."

"I promise, okay."

Trapped Between Two Mountains

That night, before she was escorted back to her cell. Gwen walked to the assistants' door and asked for a few sheets of paper and a pen to write in her diary. She also stopped by the nurses' station and repeated her request. When she came to her cell, she had collected enough paper to write several letters.

She took a deep breath and thought about her her daughter who was living with her mother in Madisonville. She had mixed feelings: torn by the feelings of being an absent mom yet relieved that she was safe and blinded from the knowledge of where her mother was.

She thought about her mother and how terrified she'd be if she knew where Gwen was. Gwen also thought about her brother, Michael and all of her siblings and the shame that they'd bare if they knew.

She thought about Blankenship's subtle threats, the disrespect of other inmates and the police confrontation. Gwen told herself that she was better than all of this and that if she found a way out, she'd never make the same mistake over and over and over again. The sentiments of these memories fueled her determination.

She finished both of the letters, she believed, just before one a.m.

Gwen, despite having few hours of sleep, awoke fresh and energized. She sat up and waited to hear the metal key engaged with her door. Gwen had placed both letters within the folds of the towel when she left the room. She received her eye drops and pills as normal. She arranged the pills underneath her tongue as she always did and drank a cup of water in front of the nurses. They waved to her to have a good day and Gwen smiled to herself as she headed toward the bathroom.

Gwen saw Linda standing off to the side with her towel. She walked by Linda and lifted up Linda's towel and put hers in its place. No words passed between the women until they saw each other in the rec room.

Gwen showed Linda how well her eyes were healing and how they hurt even less now that the swelling went down. They laughed about the men in their lives: the ones that got away and the ones they wished they could sleep with, but there was no mention of the letters.

Gwen realized that she didn't have a cigarette break yesterday. She was surprised because she realized that in of all yesterday's events, it never occurred to her that she was missing out on a smoke.

Gwen and Linda had lunch, as usual. Then they sat in the semi-circle as the assistant handed out a cigarette to each patient. Gwen took a big inhale and when she was about to exhale, someone bumped her and the cigarette fell from her hand onto the floor. She looked up and saw the wiry figure run past her. She was completely naked. She ran and leaped into the chair facing the circle. The thin woman, sat in the chair with her legs overlapping the armrest.

"OH MY GOD!" Gwen screamed, "Somebody, get her some clothes!"

Gwen looked intently at this woman and realized it was Marcia. What was Marcia doing here without any clothes? Is she allowed to roam the floor completely butt-naked, Gwen thought.

Marcia cut a striking presence. In many ways, she looked like a zombie. Her long, stringy black hair was matted and caked with dirt and oil. It was clear she hadn't had a bath in months. Her eye sockets and cheeks were sunken in. Her rib cage protruded through a thin layer of skin like a plastic wrapping over a new product. Her kneecaps looked almost deformed as her bones cracked with every movement. Her long skinny legs drifted into her long boney feet. Even her toenails were a yellowish-green.

There was no question in Gwen's mind that Marcia belonged in Western State like most of the other women she first came into contact with. But, there she sat staring at everyone with her eyes wide open playing with her private area without any concept of shame or vanity.

Gwen tried to see her story in her face but dismissed it as impossible. Gwen tapped the ashy end of her cigarette and took another puff before looking at it and exhaling.

 "Don't worry, Gwen," Linda said. *"She crazy but she's harmless. I didn't want to bother you about her because of all the other crazy women here."*

"Marcia's the one who's locked up every day except for a ten-minute break?"

"Yes. But remember to- LOOK"

Linda pointed to Marcia as Marcia had leaped off the chair and was in the face of another patient.

Marcia landed right next to the other patient and grabbed the unfinished cigarette from her and put it in her mouth. The patient started to scream and cry as she pointed to Marcia. The assistant who was standing in the doorway talking to another assistant ran over to the commotion and tried to pry the half-smoked cigarette from Marcia's mouth, but it was too late. The assistant blew the whistle that hung from his neck.

"BREAKS' OVER PATIENTS! BREAKS' OVER!"

As the women got to leave, Gwen was about to say something to Linda, when three assistants stood with their arms crossed behind her.

"Gwen Collins." One of the assistants said in a solemn voice.
"Yes?"

"Can you please come with us. We'd like to have a word with you."

Gwen looked at Linda, then back to the assistants.

"Why? Is everything alright?"

"Miss Collins, can you please come with us. We need to talk to you."

Gwen walked with the assistants but looked at Linda as she left the rec area. They walked to the nurses' station where two nurses and two assistants stood by a desk looking at her. One of the nurses walked from behind the desk. One of her hands was to her side and clenched.

"Gwen, do you know why we asked you here?"
"No. I was just having a cigarette. That's it. I wasn't involved in any incident."
"We know that and we appreciate that you've been a model patient. In the past couple of weeks, you've been nothing short of wonderful to have around here. That's why I'm so disappointed to learn that you've been deceiving us all this time."
"What do you mean? I've never lied to you."
"Yes, you have. Have you been taking the pills we've prescribed to you?"
"Yes. I take them in front of you every day."
"That's what we thought. There had to be a mistake, I asked myself, but somehow you fooled me. You fooled all of us."
"Nurse Brady, what are you talking about?"

Nurse Brady opened her hand, revealing a bunch of pills.

"These are some, the others are right there," Pointing to a small pile of pills behind her, she continued. "Do you have anything to say about this?"

Gwen stared at the pile of pills in her hand and on her desk.

"I have a right to know what you're giving me. You just can't prescribe medication for me without giving me an examination. Is this legal?"

"Miss Collins. From what we were told, you had a full physical and psychological evaluation right before you came here. I have the records,"

Brady turns around and reaches for a folder and leans against her desk.

"Here it is! This is your record from Pence. Included in this file is a detailed breakdown of your medical records. You have been prescribed medication to calm you down and to control your tendency to be disruptive. I can see from these reports that diagnosis is true. We underestimated your ability to undermine authority. We won't make that mistake again."

Gwen looked at her, then around to the other assistants, "Don't give me that bull. There was never any kind of diagnosis done at Pence. I don't have any psychological disorder. I'm being set up. Blankenship is punishing me by sending me here. Don't I get a phone call?

"Miss Collins, this is not a prison. It's a wellness institution and hospital. When we think you're ready, you'll be given that right."

"So, what are you going to do to me?"

"You give us no choice. In fact, we should have done this to begin with. We're going to give you your medicines orally now."

"No, you're not! I'm not taking them. You can't force me to take something I don't want."

"Miss Collins, you're a patient in our institution. You don't determine the course of your treatment. In fact, you're in the custody of the State of West Virginia, you've given up the right to make decisions for yourself."

Gwen started to back up but felt the body of one of the assistants behind her.

"You can't do this. I'm going to call the newspapers. I know Magistrate Carol Fouty. She won't be happy to hear that you're doing this to me."

"I'm sorry Miss Collins, but we need to give you this medication right now. And, since it's almost time for you to receive your second dose of eye drops, we'll do that as well."

"Nurse Brady, I don't want to take some stuff I don't know. I don't want to be a drug addict."

Nurse Brady nodded to the assistants behind her then walked around her desk opening a drawer and reaching for something outside of Gwen's view. Gwen, started to push and punch and kick the nearest person coming toward her. When Nurse Brady walked back, she saw Gwen held by three male assistants, one whom held her head back and locked her jaw open.

Nurse Brady took a few steps but saw that Gwen's struggle made it impossible to freely medicate her.

"HOLD HER FIRMLY. I DON'T WANT TO SPILL THIS DOSAGE."

The assistants tightened their grip on Gwen. The only freedom Gwen had was the gurgling sound that she made. It was her attempt to practice spitting from this angle. Nurse Brady squeezed the eye dropper in a small vial of liquid then put the dropper as far down Gwen's mouth as possible, then released the liquid into Gwen's throat.

"Okay, hold her still, I have three more."

After Nurse Brady finished the last dose, she walked to the water dispenser and filled the small paper cone with water and walked back to Gwen. She stopped when she saw tears streaming down the side of Gwen's face. She took a piece of tissue and tapped the tears away.

"I'm sorry, Gwen. This is for your own good. We're only following orders. I hope you'll understand the position we're in."

Then Brady slowly poured a little bit of water down Gwen's throat. Looking at the assistants,

"Keep her like that for a minutes while I get the eye drops for her. She'll be fine. In a few minutes, she won't feel like struggling."

Within five minutes, Gwen was seated in front of the nurses and the assistants with a blank stare.

"Gwen, are you ready for your eye drops?"
Gwen nodded silently.

"Very good." Nurse Brady administered the eye drops, then dabbed the extra fluids away from her face. She looked at the male assistants. "Why don't you...and you, walk Gwen back to the rec area with the other patients."

They nodded and walked Gwen back to her area in the rec hall. Linda was standing in another and ran to Gwen as she helped her to sit in her chair. Linda looked to the assistants, then looked at Gwen.

"What did they do to you?"

Gwen didn't respond. Linda looked at the assistants that were walking away.

"WHAT DID YOU DO TO HER?"

They walked away without turning around. Linda hugged Gwen. It was almost an hour before the haze of the medication began to wear off. Linda noticed Gwen looking at her for the first time since she came.

"Gwen?"
"My head and my neck hurt."
"What did they do to you?"
"I don't remember everything but they forced the medication on me. They're going to force me to drink the medication every morning."
"They can't do that to you!"
"Well, they did it."
"I'm gonna complain."
"If you do, they'll do the same to you."

Gwen turned her head slowly around while touching her neck. She looked around the room and when she saw the redhead walking around repeating her phrase on the opposite side of the room, she knew somehow that she was responsible for exposing her.

"Linda?"
"Yes, Gwen."
"Do you have the letters I wrote?"
"Yes, I have them wrapped in a dry blanket underneath my wet one. Why?"
"Mail them as soon as possible. If I don't get out of here, I'm dead."

"I'm going to mail them tomorrow. I'm going to address them to my friend and she'll get them to the mailbox immediately."

"Are you sure?"

"I'm sure. Those letters are as good as gone."

"Good. Now, I gotta find a way to minimize the effects of this medication. I can't think clearly."

A few days passed and Gwen would only remember the events of the morning a few hours after lunch. She vaguely remembered Linda telling her a couple of days before that she got the letters mailed and to be patient.

"YOU REDHEADED WHORE, YOU STOLE MY CHILDREN! YOU REDHEADED WHORE YOU STOLE MY CHILDREN"

Gwen walked past her as the woman screamed at Gwen coming out of the bathroom. Although Gwen's mind was foggy, she fought the urge to punch the woman and decided she needed to sit down and sleep.

She was entering the rec room when a woman was walking backward and almost walked into her. The woman turned around and looked at Gwen.

"DOG, DOG, DOGGIE, PETER ASSHOLE!" She said, as she pointed to Gwen and smiled. "DOG, DOG, DOGGIE, PETER ASSHOLE!"

Gwen made her way to her old spot, but on her way there she didn't see Linda. She moved a chair that was blocking the path only to see a patient kneeling on the floor holding a dead rat, shoving it in and out of her mouth. Gwen shook her head and continued to her spot.

She looked at the chair but didn't see Linda. She looked around and waited. The hours went by and Gwen began to worry about her friend. She got up and walked out in the hallway, hoping to see Linda sitting someplace or talking with someone. She just wanted to know that her friend was alright.

Gwen made it to the nurses' station where the nurses' cheerfully greeted her.

"Hi, Gwen! Is everything all right? Are you feeling sick?"
"No, I'm alright. I'm just looking for my friend, Linda."
"Linda! Gwen, Linda left early this morning. Her family came and picked her up."
"She left? She didn't say goodbye."
"I don't know if she knew or not but she checked out this morning."
"Okay. I guess I'll go back to the rec area."
"Oh, Gwen, by the way. Did you know that you have unspent commissary money?"
"Commissary money! I do! You're kidding me?"
"No. You have about $20 in commissary money in your bank account. You can spend it any way you'd like."
"Okay!"
"Just go to the window and tell them what you'd like."

Trapped Between Two Mountains

Gwen walked to the facility's store. The assistant confirmed that Gwen had money in her account but didn't know how or when the money came in. Gwen ordered a bag of chips and walked back to the rec area.

Gwen made it to her seat in the rec area and started to open the bag when another inmate heard the crinkling of the bag and came running over. Gwen saw the woman running at full speed, pushing chairs over along the way. The crazed woman got within ten feet of her, when another patient, a short woman, maybe four foot two stepped in the way.

The shorter patient put her hand out ordering the woman to stop. The running woman stopped in her tracks. The short patient put her arms on Gwen's shoulder and said:

"Don't worry, I'll protect you."

Gwen dropped the bag of chips on the floor not knowing what to do. The crazed woman stared at the bag of chips on the floor for a second then turned around and walked away, occasionally looking back to see where the chips were.

"Thank you! Oh, my god, I thought that woman was going to get me. Did you see the look in her eyes?"
"I had a nigga baby, once!"
"What! Say what!"
"I had a nigga baby, once!"
"You had a... a black baby?"

"Yes, sir. I had me my own nigga baby! But, they took him from me. That was a long, long time ago."

"You had a baby... here?"

"Sure did! My belly was out to here! And he came out of me.... right over there."

"Well, how did it happen?"

"I don't know. Well I do know something's, I just don't know how a baby can grow in you. I think my son would be about fifteen years old right about now."

"Fifteen?"

"Yeah, I'd say about fifteen. But I don't know how it happened. I was coming out of the shower and one of the men who worked here, I forgot his name, he don't work here no more, he came to me and he asked me do I want to play a game. It was fun but only he and I could play this game. So I said, sure and we played this game a lot. He said that I was the champion and that I was good at it; that made me feel real good. So, we played the game over and over again. The next thing I knew, I saw some policemen talking to him in the front and they all left. I never did see him again. That's a shame because I've been playing the game by myself ever since."

"Oh! I'm sorry to hear that."

Gwen was at a loss for words.

"Well, I'm gonna let you be. I know you have your friend who you always talk to. So, I'm gonna sit right back here in this corner and if you need me, just yell and I'll come running. I ain't scared of none of them. I'll take 'em all on. One time, I beat up *a nigga girl and a cracker one right after the other. I had blood on my fist, but I put them in their place."*

"Thank you, so much. Thank you."

"What's your name, darling?"

"My name is Gwen... and, yours?"

"Gwen... I got to remember that. That sure is a nice name. Well, I'm gonna sit over here and rest. I'll talk to you later."

Trapped Between Two Mountains

The door swung open, a few feet away West's Aunt Minerva was standing at the stove with a pot of rice on one burner, a pot of corn on another and a skillet of ground beef was cooking to a summer. Aunt Minerva looked over and saw a blur of a body run through the hallway to the boys' room.

"WEST! WEST! DON'T YOU GO MAKING A MESS IN THERE! YOU DON'T KNOW HOW LONG IT TOOK ME TO CLEAN UP THAT MESSY ROOM!"

There was no answer.

"WEST... WEST... DO YOU HEAR ME TALKIN' TO YOU?"

West was sitting on the chair across from the bunk bed. He was panting while holding his stomach. His head was bowed when Minerva walked in.

"West, what I told you about calling and letting me know where you are? You know it's getting dark earlier now and I just heard on the radio that we're supposed to have a snowstorm tonight."

"I'm sorry Auntie, I forgot. We were in town trying to get something to eat when this fella we know from school came to the same place we were at."

"That ain't no excuse for not calling. And what are you breathing so heavy for?"

"Auntie, that's what I'm trying to tell you. We were trying to get served and they took so long before we got someone to take our order. Then we had to wait, while some white people who came after us and left before us with their food. Well, we had just gotten our food and we were sitting down at a table near the drive through. That guy I was just telling you about, he's about a year or two older than us, well, he got fed up and didn't want to wait as long as we did. So, he decided he was going to ask people for money to pay for his food."

"He did what?"

"He went up to this white guy who was in his car waiting for his food to come and Richard Miller, that's the guy we know, he banged on the guy's window and said, 'Give me a dollar!' The guy told him, 'Get outta here nigga!' And the white guy rolled back up his window. Well, Richard stepped back from the guy's

car and put his foot right through the window and kicked the guy in the face!"

"Now West, tell me that you didn't get into a fight for that fool?"

"No, Auntie, we got up and ran. We left half of our food there. When we heard the police coming, we took off. We left him there. He stood there shouting that he ain't leaving! When we came up the road, we saw him in the back of a squad car cussing and carrying on."

"Now, West, why didn't you just leave when you saw them give you bad service? Your money is green, too. It'll spend just like white folks' money will spend. Money don't care whose pocket it's in as long as it's being passed around."

"Auntie, listen... we didn't know the guy was gonna take that long and when we finally decided to leave, that's when all of the stuff with Richard Miller went down. We left and ran all the way here."

Minerva had her arms crossed and stared at West for a couple of seconds.

"West, I promised your mother I would take care of you. How would it look or what would I say to her if something happened to you?"

"I know Auntie. I promise you, we weren't looking for any trouble. I'm a lover, not a fighter."

Minerva looked at him with a side eye,

Trapped Between Two Mountains

"A lover, Huh? I guess I gotta keep my eye on you, lover."

Then she turned around and walked out of the bedroom, but continued to talk to West as she went back to the kitchen.

"West!"

"Yes, Auntie!"

"I forgot to tell you. Your cousin was looking for you all afternoon. He wanted to know if he could borrow your bike. I told him that he'd have to wait until you came home, but he was with his friends. So after the third time he came, I let him borrow your bike so he wouldn't walk while everybody else was riding. I didn't think you'd mind. By the way, every time I look at that bike it looks different. I can't put my finger on it."

"No," West yelled from his room. "That's alright. I would have given it to him myself."

West woke up the next morning and heard his cousin snoring in the bunk beneath him. He didn't hear when he came into the house, much less when he came into the room.

West got out of bed and looked out the window. He saw his bike leaned up against the side of the house. He was thrown a loop for a second: his bike seat was different. West pressed his face against the glass looking for his seat. In its place was a long bone-colored Schwinn banana seat. Was it his bike? Did his cousin pick up the wrong bike by accident? Some parts of the bike looked like West's, but others didn't. Last week, his cousin brought back the bike, but the handles were different. These handles flared out like a chopper. Now, this same bike has a different seat, a cooler looking seat, West thought.

West stood at the window smiling. The bike was now growing on him. He was becoming fond of its look. If this was in fact his bike, he would have bragging rights over all the kids in the neighborhood. He would be the cat's meow, as they say.

Thoughts of West racing down the hill filled his mind. West saw the reflection of himself grinning in the window. He turned to see if his cousin was awake to ask him if this was his bike because if it wasn't, he wanted it, even if he had to buy it. His cousin was partially turned over but was still asleep. West turned back to the window to see two faces looking back at him.

"Oh, my god! You scared me. What're you guys doing here? Don't you know what time it is?" West said as he put his hand on his heart.

Dickie Johnson made a face in the window and Michael Mosely stood a bit off and said nothing as usual.

West raised up the window and felt the cool air come in. He brushed the snow that piled up against the outside of the glass outwards.

"If I knew any better, I would throw you two right in that snow," West said, while not wanting to let them know he was glad to see them.

"What you guys doing here anyway? I was just about to get a bowl of Cap'n Crunch."

"Well, then get me a bowl while you at it. Mosely don't eat that cause his grandparents would kill him!"

"I know you didn't come over here to eat my food when you know your cartoons are on. What you want!"

"West... the snow is good out here. Let's go and race before the snow starts to melt."

"Dickie that can wait. I'm still a little sore from running home from Shoney's last night. You heard what happened, right?"

"Yeah, I heard about Miller. That fool needs to be locked up. Look West, this is the best time to race. The snow is white, white. In a few hours, it'll be gray and slushy. You hesitant cause you afraid I might beat you like I always do."

"Boy, don't start that. I gotta whole lotta whipping for you. I was just thinking about racing down the alley with my new bike."

"Man, we can race down the alley anytime. You know how long we gotta wait for this kind of snow?"

West looked over Dickie's shoulder and saw white, sparkling snow reflecting the early morning sun like light off a diamond. Then West thought for a minute, if he could beat "Big Mouth Dickie" down the hill, he could make him buy lunch for the week and that also means that West could save up his lunch money for something else.

Trapped Between Two Mountains

"You know what Dickie, you're on. I'll meet you out in the front in five minutes. I gotta get my sled out the back. I ain't had it out since I kicked your butt last year."

"A lot has changed in a year. You see a growing a mustache, you... you still ain't even got a little peach fuzz to show."

West waved him off then looked at Michael.

"What's Michael here for?"

"He wants to race, too."

"What!" Looking at Michael, "You serious, you came here cause you wanna race? Your granddad and grandma know you outside?"

"I ain't serving time. They let me go out when I wanna go out. I don't take no orders." Michael said, with an expressionless face.

"Okay.... Okay. I'm glad to hear that. Well, that makes two of y'all that's gonna owe me money." Dickie laughed.

"West, you still owe me money from last week."

"Well, now you gonna owe me money. Just meet me out in the front in five minutes and make sure you got your money ready."

West, Dickie and Michael pulled their sleighs from in front of Aunt Minerva's house. They normally didn't ride or race down the alley directly in front of her house because they weren't ready to get a butt-whoopin' for acting stupid.

Trapped Between Two Mountains

They normally passed the second alley, which was called, The Church Alley. This is because in the church on that street, the windows had eyes; and there was always a lot of confessing, even if it was someone else's sins.

They made it to the third street down. This was the alley that was every bicyclist's, every sleigh rider's and every skateboarder's dream: nothing but a street all the way down until you got to the railroad tracks by the Kanawha River. Only the Big Boys attempted such a feat, little boys had to stay up the hill.

West and Dickie didn't say anything until they got to the Third Alley. This was when they spend all of their pent-up braggings for the actual race. Michael followed behind saying nothing.

All of them fixed their coats and tied their sneaker laces very, very tight. West pulled on his knit gloves, while Dickie rubbed his hands on his jeans.

"I don't need gloves. Men don't need gloves, West. That's the difference between you and me. I got hair on my chest and you all you got is that nappy head of yours."

"You gotta got a big mouth. Why don't you put your money where your mouth is!"

"Yeah, what you got?"

West looked at him, then grinned.

"Why don't we double it?"

"Double it? West, you ain't got no money. You hummin' and bummin' for money all the time. I know you got those white girls buying your school lunch. That ain't happening here."

"Why, you scared?"

"No. I just know you ain't got nothin' to offer."

"I dare you to take my bet. In fact, I double dare you."

"West, I could buy all of your clothes and still get change back from a five dollar bill."

"You tellin' me you scared. You know what, just for that, I triple-dog-dare you. If you're really as good as you say you are, you'd take me up."

Dickie grinned to himself and looked at West's sleigh. He liked how West's sleigh performed the year before and was tempted to make West an offer for it.

"I'll tell you what. I accept that bet and when I win, I want your sleigh."

"My sleigh?"

"Yeah, your sleigh."

West stared at him for a second.

"Okay. You on. What about Michael."

"Michael is just here to witness me kicking your butt."

No, I ain't. I got my sleigh, too. I'm here to show you I'm good, too."

West and Dickie turned to look at the hill without responding.

Trapped Between Two Mountains

"Okay, I got my spot. Where you standing, Dickie?" West asked.

"I... I'm gonna stand... right here."

"Michael find a spot, but not too close to either of us."

West, Dickie and Michael set their sleighs about five feet apart from each other, neither West nor Dickie looked at Michael when they started the countdown. Both of them made non-verbal gestures to the other about winning.

The countdown from ten went quick but West felt the adrenaline as he never had before. The stakes of a hearty lunch and after school bites at the local restaurant was too exciting not to think about, but he also realized that he could lose his sleigh: one of his favorite Christmas gifts.

They looked at each other at the last second, then pushed off.

The pure white snow, which covered the road and a few cars parked along the side flew between the boys like waves made by surfboards when the tides come in. But, this was no open sea, they were battling each other and the laws of gravity.

The soft snow felt like little daggers as it was lifted and propelled by the force of their speed. Every few seconds, West and Dickie would turn to the side to see where the other was. Neither wanted the other to have even an inch lead on the other. This often meant tucking their bodies closer to the sled, almost being parallel.

Then something interesting happened insomuch that both West and Michael forgot about winning. It was the sound of something crossing the street just two blocks ahead of them. Both of them wanted to end the race at a point where their sled was just beyond the other, but neither agreed.

Finally, West screamed out:

"WE GOTTA STOP, THERE'S A CAR CROSSING. WE CAN'T MAKE IT."

Dickie heard the same sound getting louder and he waved from West to turn to the side in one direction, and he in the other. Both of them spun out. When they came to themselves and looked at one another, they were not worse for the wear. In back of them, Michael was about ten feet back and was now closing in.

"MICHAEL... MICHAEL... STOP... TURN OFF!" Dickie screamed to the sleigh rider that just flew past him and West.

"TURN THE HANDLE, MICHAEL! TURN THE HANDLE!" West shouted.

West and Dickie saw Michael struggling to get the sleigh under control but he was going too fast and he didn't know how to stop. The sleigh turned slightly but now Michael was headed for a parked truck. West closed his eyes as he heard Dickie futilely scream out directions.

West opened his eyes and saw Michael hit the bumper on the truck and get knocked off of the sleigh. The sleigh, unmanned, flew underneath the truck and came out on the other side to a rest about five feet away.

There was silence between West and Dickie after they heard the loud thump of Michael's head against the truck. Michael got up and brushed himself off. He didn't turn to West and Dickie but walked around the truck and picked up his sleigh.

He came around the truck and had a huge bump the size of an orange in the middle of his forehead. He didn't say anything to them, but started the long journey back up the hill.

"Michael, are you okay?" West and Dickie would ask frequently as they followed him up the hill. Michael wouldn't say anything.

Dickie and West looked at each other in amazement. For a moment, they both thought that they underestimated Michael. They walked a few feet away from Michael and followed him as he approached his grandparent's house. It was clear Michael didn't want to say anything to them and was finished for the day, but they were still concerned. The welt had grown even more.

West and Dickie stood just outside of Michael's gate when he went through. Michael turned around, tight-lipped and then turned to the front door and knocked. The door opened a minute later and Michael's grandmother stood in the doorway. She saw Michael standing there but was unaware of his condition until she put on her glasses to see her grandson. West and Michael were about thirty feet away. They watched her expression change from sleepy to terrified.

Michael dropped his sleigh and threw his hands up up to his head. "WHAAAAAAAAAH! WHAAAAAAAAAAHHHHHHHHHHHH!

WHAAAAAAAHHHHH!

West and Dickie ran home without turning back. They ignored the sound of Michael's grandmother calling for them. West ran in the house and peeked out the side of the living-room curtain. He saw the ambulance in front of Michael's home and the medics walking Michael to the van with some kind of compress on his head.

"West! What are you doing?" Aunt Minerva said as she walked into the living-room.
"Nothing, Auntie. Just looking at the snow."

Minerva walked to the window beside West.

"West, you see that? What's happening over there? Is that your friend?"
"Auntie, I see but I don't know what happened to him."
"Lord, that boy was probably doing something he knew he wasn't supposed to do. Lord, help these kids, cause I can't."

Minerva turned and walked back into her bedroom and closed the door.

Gwen laid in her bed. A few hours later she was still staring at the ceiling. It was the first time since she came to Western State that she felt alone. It surprised her but even in those times when one friend would leave, another one would show up and she didn't have to compromise herself. The idea fascinated her and she began to see a correlation between friendships that just happen and friendships that she tried to make on her own. She closed her eyes. She had a lot to rethink.

There was a hard knock on Gwen's door, then the metal key went into the slot. At first, Gwen thought it was a dream, but, someone was trying to get into her room and get into it very fast. The door swung open and one of the morning nurses stuck her head in. Her face was pale as if she had just seen a ghost.

"COLLINS! COLLINS... GET UP. GET UP, NOW!"

"What's happening. Why are you shouting? I'm right here."

"Get dressed and gather all of your belongings. Put all of them neatly in one pile on your bed and follow me."

"Where are we going? I've been taking the medications. What more do you want?"

"Collins, this is no time to get into a discussion about your treatments. I need for you to take a shower, comb your hair and brush your teeth. We have a meeting in ten minutes. Let's go."

Gwen got up and slowly gathered her things. She put all of her clean clothes in one pile and the worn stuff, folded in another pile. She grabbed a clean towel and her toothbrush and followed the nurse to the shower. When they got to the bathroom, there was a janitor in there quickly mopping the floor and wiping down the sink. The patients were told to hurry up and finish their business and report to the rec room.

"Collins, unless you need to use the toilet, I need you to get into the shower right now."

The nurse helped Gwen get her things together after she came out of the shower and looked at her to make certain she looked presentable.

"What's this all about? Why are you talking to me?"

"Collins, we have some people here to see you. They're here to inspect your living conditions and to make sure you're all right. We've treated you fairly and have been nothing but nice to you from the day you came to our facility. And, I expect that is what you'll tell them if they should ask."

"Tell who? Who are you talking about?"

"You don't' know? Have you spoke with anyone outside of our facility?"

"I can't even get a phone call to my mother and you're asking me about some strangers?"

The nurse looked into Gwen's eyes and realized that she was right. She walked Gwen to the nurses' station and had her seated there. Nurse Brady came running from the assistants' office to her desk and she went rummaging through her file cabinet before running back to their office.

Gwen stood up and saw two neatly dressed women in business suits and a man in a shirt and tie. They all held leather briefcases and they seemed to be having a heated argument, or at least that is what their non-verbal gestures through the glass were saying to Gwen.

"Can I get you some water, Gwen?" The first nurse asked.

"Yes, thank you. Who are those people? Are these the strangers you're worried about?"

The nurse handed Gwen a cup of water. Gwen looked up and saw the guests in the room looking through the door's window directly at her, then resumed their heated discussion with Nurse Brady and the staff. It was less than five minutes later that the two women followed by the man walked quickly to Gwen.

"Gwen Collins?"

"Yes, ma'am. Are you here to see me? Did I do something wrong? I've been swallowing the medicine they've been putting in my mouth."

"Oh, really! Well, Miss Collins, first let me introduce ourselves. My name is Miss Cunningham, she's Miss Montgomery and he's Mr. Berry. And we're from the Appalachian Research and Defense Fund. We're here because we're investigating reports of abuse by the staff on patients here. We believe from talking with Nurse Brady, that you and another inmate.... Braxton was sent here illegally and forced to take illegal sedatives. We'd like to represent you against the Western State and Pence State for endangerment and false imprisonment. Would you like us to proceed in this matter as your counsel?"

Gwen started crying.

"I've been praying for someone to come and see what they've been doing to me and my friend, Buffy. We don't belong here. Some policemen sprayed us with mace and they beat us. My eyes are still a bit swollen and I may even have a permanent scar right here in my forehead. Could you help us? Oh, by the way, they've been holding my mouth open every morning and pouring something down my throat and I told them that I've never even been checked by a doctor."

"We're well aware of that and many, many other violations of yours and Braxton's civil liberties. We're going to get this resolved as soon as possible. The staff knows that it is illegal for them to give you anymore medications and if they do, you let us know and we'll take it from there."

"Miss Cunningham, when are me and Buffy going to get out?"

"We're working on that right now. Don't be surprised if a reporter or two shows up here to interview you. They have a right to speak to you and if the staff tried to prevent you from talking, just call us.... Mr. Berry, do you have a business card for her? Good. Okay, you see this number here? You can reach any of us by this number. If we're not in, we'll get back to you as soon as possible."

"Please don't leave."

"Don't worry. They won't try anything. We'll be back to see you in a few days."

The two women and the gentleman walked past Nurse Brady and the staff without saying anything, but turned to Gwen from the door and nodded. The first security door closed behind them.

"I see you found a way to have your voice heard, Collins. I don't know how you did it, but you did. Now, you're a problem that Pence will have to deal with."

Nurse Brady looked at one of the male assistants.

"You and you, take Collins back to her room and make certain she has all of her belongings in order."

It should have been a moment of victory, but when Gwen sat on the bed she was terrified. Terrified at the thought of what might happen next. Terrified that before the lawyers came back, the staff would have already done something mean to her. Terrified at the thought of dealing with Warden Blankenship. She realized that she was trapped between two mountains. And, both were a very steep climb.

Gwen's door was unlocked when she fell asleep on the bed, but she heard another hard knock on the door. She opened her eyes and her blurry vision cleared to see Officer Crawford standing in the doorway.

"COLLINS... COLLINS, GET UP! YOU HAVE TWO MINUTES TO GATHER ALL OF YOUR THINGS."

Gwen's heart raced but she forgot the stiffness of her joints and threw all of her things in a pillowcase and walked to the door. Crawford handcuffed her and held Gwen's pillowcase in her free hand. They walked through double-security, self-locking doors to the front of the building. Officer Jones, who was waiting in the front with Buffy, handed Crawford the facilities records detailing Gwen's behavior. Crawford took it with the hand that held the pillowcase and all four women walked through the doors of Western State.

Trapped Between Two Mountains

In the cool evening night, Gwen and Buffy were in the backseat leaning against each other as the car drove off the estate and onto the highway back to Pence Springs.

Trapped Between Two Mountains

Te estas ahogando en un vaso de agua
[You can drown in a glass of water]

– Spanish proverb

Trapped Between Two Mountains

"Being from the area Ms. Collins was born,
I enjoyed her book immensely as I knew some of the people mentioned,
Could not put this book or Book ONE down until I finished them.
It ended too soon!

I do hope she continues her books and show how her life continued
...and if she ever got her life back on track."

-- RanRan
Customer review on Amazon

Praises For ONE

"...I'm not brave, but after reading A Journey Begins, I said to myself, I too have a journey. A lot different from you but a pretty wild one.... I have to read book TWO cause I'm looking forward to reading about more about Jink. I have to find out about the jerks you ran from."
-- marty.holley@

"Chapter 6 was enlightening. Chapter 6 was very emotional for me. I was saddened to learn that a person in the neighborhood that everyone knew and trusted was molesting the children."
--An Amazon reader

www.ingramcontent.com/pod-product-compliance
Lightning Source LLC
Chambersburg PA
CBHW020121130526
44591CB00031B/277